LITTLE BOY BRAVE

Peggy Holloway

Cover designed by Patti Roberts

Of Paradox

Book Covers, Promotions and Trailer

Productions

Pattiroberts7@gmail.com

http://paradoxbooktrailerproductions.blogspoy.

com.au/

CHAPTER 1

They were fighting again. He couldn't take it. He had to get out. He was only eight years old, but he had to leave. He was going to take care of himself. Throwing everything into his duffle bag, and unzipping his small tent, Billy crawled out and stood listening.

"Why do you always have to drink? We can't even go camping without you bringing a bottle?" That was Daddy talking. Mama was a drunk. She was mean. She sometimes hit Billy and screamed at him.

"Oh, shut up! You sound like a baby. It's your fault anyway. You would drive a nun to drink, always on me about something."

"Keep your voice down. You'll wake Billy. This camping trip was supposed to be something to bring our family together. It was your idea. 'Let's take Billy camping, Kenny. Let's get away, get out into nature. It'll be good for us,'" he mimicked.

"And we did. Billy had a good time today, fishing with you and cooking the fish over an open fire. Didn't we have fun swimming in the lake together, as a family? I don't understand what your problem is. I like to have a little drink in the evenings, so what?"

"Come off it, Rose! You don't like to have a little drink in the evening. No, you like to get drunk and sloppy every night. And then you get mean. You're not the woman I married, Rose."

"You're not the woman I married, Rose," she mimicked. "You think you're the man I married? Look at you! You're fat and bald and you can't even earn a decent living. We can't even have a real house, living in a trailer, oh, excuse me, I mean a double wide. And, by the way, where have you been getting loving from, huh? Where? Who is she?"

"Quit shoving me, Rose. This is what I was talking about when I said you get mean. Do you really think I want to make love to someone who smells like you every night? And look at you. You've let yourself go. Before we got married, you kept your body fit. You did aerobics every day; you wouldn't eat any processed foods. What happened to you, Rose?"

"You happened to me, Kenny. You! What you see here is the end result of marrying a slob and having to put up with his brat."

"I told you to keep your voice down!" Slap!

"Now comes the hitting," Billy thought. "First comes the blaming and then comes the hitting."

Billy took his tent down trying not to make any noise. Rolling it up, he stuffed it in his duffle bag. And then he ran.

CHAPTER 2

Once, when Billy was little, his daddy took him camping. They fished, swam in the lake, and hiked in the hills. This was their special place they had found, a place to camp out together. Daddy had taught him a lot about survival. That was before he married Rose. She was so nice at first, insisting on him calling her Mama.

Billy never knew his real mama. Daddy had told him that his Mama had died in child birth. Billy always felt guilty about that.

Billy now knew what to do. He could live on his own. He could catch his own fish and kill his own rabbits and squirrels. He'd be like an Indian, except he would build him a house. No one would hit him ever again.

As he climbed higher and higher into the hills, Billy began to feel sad. He was going to miss his dad. His dad had never hit him. They were pals before Rose came along. He was going to miss his bike and he was going to miss Sandy. Sandy was his best friend. She lived in the trailer park next to Billy. They had played together since they were little. Sandy's parents were nice. Her mama made cookies for them and gave them Kool-Aid. He used to wish he could live with Sandy and her family.

Impatiently, Billy wiped a tear from his cheek. "One day, when I'm grown, I'll go back and marry Sandy," he said.

Billy decided that if he didn't want anyone to find him, he would have to get off the hiking trail. Shining his flashlight up into the forest above him, Billy left the trail and hiked toward the top of the hill. It was much more difficult to hike straight up like that. He kept sliding on the pine needles. They were thick and slick. As the hill got steeper, he pulled himself up by holding onto small trees.

He was tired when he got to the top. Shining his flashlight on his Mickey Mouse watch, Billy was surprised at the time. It was after midnight. He had been hiking for almost five hours. He was proud that he could pitch his tent by himself. When he got the tent up and relieved himself behind a tree, he crawled inside his sleeping bag. As he was dozing, he smiled to himself and mumbled, "They won't miss me til morning."

CHAPTER 3

Rose woke up the next morning with a whopper of a headache. She wanted to go back to sleep but she had to pee real badly. This was a bad idea, this camping trip. It would have been better if they had rented a space in a regular campground. Then she wouldn't have to go in the woods. She envied men sometimes. They could pee in the woods so easily. She was always so scared that she would hover over poison ivy and get an itchy crotch.

Rose stumbled out of the tent and headed for the woods. Crouching behind a tree, she glanced around, nervously. When she finished, she took a tissue out of her jeans pocket and blotted herself. It was cold this morning. She rushed back to the tent, grabbed a sweatshirt, and pulled it over her tee. Kenny was snoring loudly. He looked like a beached whale. Standing there staring at Kenny, Rose wondered why she had married him.

This was her fourth marriage. She had come to the conclusion that most men were losers. A few women were lucky enough to get the good ones. Those women didn't have to drink. Kenny couldn't see that, if he would be the kind, loving, husband she thought she had married, then she wouldn't have to drink. Then she could remember what happened the night before.

Shaking her head in disgust, Rose sat down on her sleeping bag, grabbed her purse, and got out her compact.

"You son-of-a-bitch," she screamed when she saw yet another black eye.

"Huh?" Attempting to jump out of bed, Kenny forgot he was zipped inside a sleeping bag. He thought at first that Rose had tied him to the bed.

"Come on, Rose, untie me," he said.

She laughed. "What the hell are you doing, Kenny? Just unzip the damn bag." She shook her head. "What a moron."

"Is Billy up yet?" he said, yawning.

"How would I know?"

"I thought you had already been outside."

"I have, but I didn't see him up and about."

Kenny unzipped the tent and crawled out. Glancing to his left, his mind didn't, at first, take in what he was seeing. He did a double take and then his heart sped up. Billy's tent was gone.

"Rose!" he yelled to the top of his lungs.

"What?" she asked, coming out of the tent. "Quit yelling. You're giving me a headache."

She stood beside him looking around. "Where's Billy?"

"That's what I'd like to know. Was his tent here when you came out before?"

She nodded. "Yeah, it was here. He can't be far."

Before she got the sentence out, Kenny started running toward the hills, yelling for Billy.

Rose watched him, hoping Billy was lost. She honestly couldn't remember seeing the tent there when she went to pee. If she told Kenny, he would hit her again. She watched Kenny running up the hiking trail. Then she went back into the tent to get makeup to cover her black eye. She looked at her watch. It was 10:27 a.m.

CHAPTER 4

Billy had been up since seven. Studying his compass, he had decided to head south and east. He had been living in Tennessee and thought he would go live in Florida. It would be easier to live in the woods in Florida, even in the winter. He had packed all his gear and hiked down the side of the hill, going southeast.

Coming to another hill, he started up. There were hills as far as he could see. It was now almost 11:00 a.m. and Billy was getting hungry. He wished he had grabbed some of the groceries from the boxes sitting on the picnic table. At least he had remembered to take his canteen. There had been several crystal clear streams where he had filled it. Water wasn't a problem.

Hearing voices off in the distance, Billy stopped to listen.

"Did you catch any fish, Harry?" he heard a woman say.

A man laughed. "I caught more than we'll ever eat, Katrina. Where's Megan?"

"She went for another swim. I don't see how in the world she can swim in that cold water."

The man laughed. "You swam in ice cold water when you were eight years old, I'll bet."

"You're right. You don't notice the cold when you're a kid."

Billy sneaked up on the happy couple, but hid behind a tree. He watched as they laughed and talked together. Circling around their campsite, going from tree to tree, Billy came to a lake. There was a little girl playing in the water.

She giggled. "Quit nibbling my toes, little fishes."

Suddenly, becoming very still, she called out, "Who's there?" She turned in a complete circle and then stopped. She was looking at the tree where Billy was hiding.

"I can see you," she said. "Who are you? Come on out."

Billy came out from behind the tree while glancing over his shoulder toward the campsite. It was higher than the lake so that Billy could only see the top of her parents' heads.

Megan studied Billy and then said, "You ran away from home?" She walked out of the lake, grabbing a towel from the dock.

While drying herself off, she said, "What's your name?"

"I'm Billy and you're Megan. We're both the same age."

When she looked surprised, he laughed. "I heard your parents talking. By the way, they have more fish than y'all can eat. You think you could bring me some when it gets ready?"

She grinned. "I'll bring you some tonight, after they've gone to bed. Why did you run away?"

"My daddy married a witch, with a capital B."

Megan thought a moment and then laughed. "You're funny," she said.

#####

Billy stretched out on a bed of pine needles and waited for the fish. He could smell the delicious fried cornmeal aroma and his mouth watered, then his stomach growled. He looked at his watch. It was only seven fifteen. Wondering what time they would go to bed, he was soon sound asleep.

"Billy," Megan said in a loud whisper.

Billy had been dreaming that he was at home and that his step mama was hitting him. He jumped up, looking around wild-eyed. When he saw Megan, he smiled.

"I brought you some food," she whispered, handing him a large paper bag.

Billy opened the bag. Inside was a large Ziploc bag filled with fish and hushpuppies, a plastic container of Cole slaw, a plastic fork, and a stack of paper napkins.

Megan watched as Billy opened each container, closing his eyes as he tasted each item. He ate only one piece of fish, one hushpuppy and one third of the slaw. After wiping his mouth on one of the napkins, he put everything back in the bag and put the bag into his backpack.

"Well, I'd better get going," Billy said, looking at his watch. He was glad to see that it was only nine fifteen. "Thanks," he said as he stood and put on his backpack.

"Where ya goin?" Megan asked.

"To Florida."

"Wish I could go with you."

Without another word, and without looking back, Billy walked off. Megan watched until he was out of sight.

"Wish I could go to Florida," she said and sighed.

CHAPTER 5

"Damn that kid," Rose mumbled under her breath, as she continued up the hiking trail. "I hope he dies out here. Yeah, I hope we find his dead body. He has been nothing but trouble since I first laid eyes on him."

"Come on, Rose," Kenny yelled over his shoulder. "It'll be dark soon. We need to find my boy."

They had been hiking all day and Rose was cold, tired, hungry, and angry. She hoped they never found the little brat. She wondered how much longer Kenny would search before giving up. Suddenly Kenny stopped, causing Rose to bump into the back of him. He turned around and shoved her. Rose fell on her butt and let out a yelp. Before Rose could complain, Kenny put his finger to his lips, signaling her to keep quiet. Rose smelled fried fish and her stomach growled. Then she heard laughter.

"Daddy, that's not true!" a little's girl's voice said, giggling.

"Who's out there?" the man's voice said.

Rose and Kenny came out of the woods and into the camping area.

"We're looking for my boy," Kenny said. "We were camping out on the other side of the hill, that is, two hills over. He's been missing since this morning."

Harry got up and shook hands with Kenny. "You folks sit down and have a cup of coffee. You must be plum worn out. Any coffee left, Kat?"

Katrina put two more cups on the table and filled them with coffee. "Y'all hungry? We got plenty a fish left over." She put two paper plates on the table and started filling them.

Kenny and Rose ate like they were starving. They hadn't taken time to eat before taking off on their search.

"Have you seen my boy?" Kenny asked between mouthfuls.

"No, we've seen no one besides ourselves."

As Harry said this, Kenny noticed Megan drop her head. She stared down at the ground.

"How about you, little lady?" Kenny said, looking at Megan.

Megan felt herself blush. Both of her parents were looking at her.

"Me-gan?" her mom said. "Did you see him?"

Megan shook her head but didn't reply.

"Megan," her father demanded harshly, "if you know anything about this, you need to tell these folks. They're worried about their little boy."

"He was here last night. I gave him some of our left over fish," Megan said looking from one adult to another.

Rose looked at Kenny and he looked like he wanted to kill her. She knew he would hit her when they were alone again. She had lied to him about seeing the tent that morning.

"Damn," Kenny said. "He's already got a twenty four hour head start. Did he say where he intended on going, Megan?"

"No," she lied. She liked Billy. She didn't want him to have to live with his step mama.

Megan's mama bent down, her eyes level with her daughter's. "Megan, are you telling the truth? The poor child could get hurt out there. Wouldn't you feel bad if he got hurt?"

"But I don't know where he went, Mama, honest," Megan said while crossing

20

her fingers behind her back. She forced herself to look her mama in the eye.

"Okay, I believe you, honey," her mama said. She stood and started cleaning up the dishes. Rose sat watching her without offering to help.

"Where are you guys camping out?" Harry asked Kenny.

"Just on the other side of Logan's Run."

"That's not far from the ranger's station. Why don't I run you over there so they can get a search party together?"

CHAPTER 6

Billy had walked as far as he could from Megan's family. Finding a level spot, he pitched his tent and ate one of the hushpuppies. After relieving himself, he crawled into his sleeping bag. His illuminated watch showed 1:45 a.m. He was asleep as soon as his head touched the pillow.

What woke Billy up was the sound of crunching. It sounded like an animal was eating, chewing very loudly. He had brought his small supply of food inside the tent, so it couldn't be his food. Billy got out of his sleeping bag. Lying on the floor of the tent, he unzipped the bottom few inches of the flap.

A Black Bear was munching on an apple. Billy smiled to himself. According to his daddy, Black Bears weren't aggressive, not like Grizzly Bears.

"So, there are apples growing somewhere around here," Billy mumbled to himself.

His stomach growled. Pulling a piece of fish out of his backpack, he unzipped the tent all the way and ate, while watching the bear. After the bear wondered off, Billy zipped the tent and crawled back into the sleeping bag. A few hours later, he woke up cold. Curling into a ball, he tried to get comfortable, but couldn't. He decided to break camp and make some more miles.

When Billy was ready to go, he looked around for an apple tree. Spotting one off to the left he filled his backpack. As he was running downhill, along a switchback, Billy turned a sharp corner and came face to face with the bear. The trail was both steep and narrow at this point. Billy lost his balance and fell off the trail. Sliding down the side of the hill, his back pack got caught on a branch and was jerked off his shoulders. He was moving too fast to stop, and retrieve it.

As he accelerated, Billy's small frame turned sideways, and then upside down so that he was sliding head first. His head hit a boulder, stopping Billy, knocking him unconscious.

CHAPTER 7

The search party never found Billy. They searched for three days before Rose and Kenny went back to Nashville and reported his disappearance to the police. The police questioned them, separately. The police would have suspected foul play, if they hadn't questioned Megan and her family. They put out an Amber Alert.

Kenny slammed the truck into gear and peeled out of the parking lot, leaving the police station. Rose watched him. She knew he would blame her for Billy's disappearance.

Neither one spoke until they reached home. Screeching to a stop under the carport, inches from the house, Kenny turned to Rose. His eyes were wild when he looked at her. Rose opened the car door. Before she could get out, he grabbed her hair, dragging her across the seat, banging her head on the steering wheel.

"You bitch! You're glad he's gone, aren't you? I can see it in your eyes. You hope he never comes home."

"Stop, you bastard. Stop!" she cried, while trying to pull her hair from his grasp. Her head felt like it would explode any minute. Tears streamed down her face. She needed a drink.

Kenny continued to hit her head on the steering wheel. "If anything happens to Billy, I'll kill you, you no good cunt." He finally quit smashing her head and shoved her away. "Get in the house!"

Rose tried to open the car door, but was shaking so badly she couldn't get it opened. Kenny got out and walked into the back yard. Lighting a cigarette, he stared at the swing set he had put up four years ago. Tears began to slide down his face. He loved his boy. Billy was the only decent thing in Kenny's life. He didn't love Rose. He didn't know if he had ever loved her. When they had started dating, she had appeared to be such a loving, caring, person. Kenny thought Billy needed a mother. He felt like he couldn't be both mother and father to Billy.

"I messed up," Kenny said to himself, as he crushed his cigarette butt out on the ground. "It's all Rose's fault that Billy ran away. I'm going to kill her. I'm really going to kill her."

Rose had managed to get the car door opened and stood in the kitchen looking out the window at Kenny. He was walking around talking to himself.

"Damn stupid bastard," she said. She opened the cabinet above the sink, pulled down a bottle of vodka, and poured herself a full glass with no ice. Closing her eyes, she drank the whole glass without stopping. Taking a deep breath, she poured another glass. Continuing to watch Kenny, Rose drank, enjoying the burn as the vodka slid down her throat. By the time Kenny came in the back door, Rose didn't really care what he did.

Kenny took one look at Rose, the glass, and the bottle of vodka and his blood boiled. Grabbing the bottle, he hit her with it. The bottle broke and her forehead was cut and bleeding. She slid down the cabinet and sat dazed on the floor. Kenny looked around for something else to hit her with and noticed the iron skillet on the stove. It still had bacon grease since the morning they had left for the camping trip.

Rose looked up at Kenny, stupidly, as he swung the skillet with all of his strength, hitting her square in the face. She fell over and lay on the floor. The rage that had been building since his marriage to Rose took over so that Kenny was unaware of what he was doing. When he finally gained control of his senses, Kenny stared down at her. He couldn't believe he had done it. He had killed Rose.

CHAPTER 8

"Maw! Hey, Maw, the boy's coming to. Open your eyes, boy."

When Billy opened his eyes, he saw the meanest looking man he had ever seen. The man had black eyes, set close together, and black greasy hair that looked like it had never been washed or combed. He smiled down at Billy. He had only four yellow teeth. His left eye went off to the left.

Billy was lying on a narrow cot that stank of human sweat, urine, and something else Billy couldn't identify. He was covered with a threadbare blanket. There were no sheets on the bed and no pillowcase on the pillow. He was in a shack.

"Git away from him, Elvis," an old snaggled tooth woman said.

She came in carrying a bowl of soup. Elvis backed away, eyeing his mama, as if he thought she was going to hit him. With thinning gray hair, pulled into a knot at the top of her head, Billy thought she looked like a kindly old grandma. Billy had never met any of his grandparents and didn't know if he had any. His daddy refused to talk about his parents. Billy didn't want to know Rose's parents.

Sitting on the edge of the bed, the old woman smiled at Billy. "Glad you woke up, finally. Here, let's git some soup inside ya."

She dipped a huge spoon into the bowl of soup and moved it towards Billy's mouth. He eyed it suspiciously, but, when he sipped from the edge of the spoon, it was delicious.

"It's vegetable beef," she said, giving him another spoon full. "What's your name?"

"Billy." He looked at Elvis, who was lighting a corncob pipe. Billy laughed. He had heard about corn cob pipes, but didn't think anyone ever really used them.

The old woman smiled at him, showing her three teeth. "How'd you come to be out thor in our backyard?"

"I was hiking and fell down the hill. How long have I been here?"

"Thirteen days. I patched you up the best I could. We'll have ole doc look yer over when he gets here on Thursday. He's coming in to look at old Bessie, our mule. She's been sick. He should be here in a few days. We'll git him to call your parents too.

He has one of them cell phones. They must be worriet sick about ya."

"No!" Billy said.

"No? What do you mean no?"

"I don't want you to call my parents. I don't want to live with them anymore."

The old woman eyed him and then nodded. "I see. It's like that is it? Ya run away?"

Billy nodded.

"Well, we'll see," she said.

Billy knew when a grownup said, "we'll see," then they usually did what they wanted to do, not what the kid wanted them to do. He would have to leave here as soon as they went to sleep. What Billy didn't know was the hot chocolate Maw had given him just before bedtime was laced with a small amount of whiskey. It wasn't much, but it was enough to make a small boy like Billy sleep deeply.

The next morning, the woman named Maw brought Billy a bowl of oatmeal. Billy hated oatmeal, but made himself eat it so he would be strong. Maw helped him get to the outhouse. He didn't see her around when he finished his business in there, so he weakly walked back toward the shack. On the way Billy saw a skinny man with a doctor's bag come out of one of the outbuildings. He was talking to Maw and he looked serious. Maw waved Billy over.

Maw introduced him to Dr. Ethane. The doctor picked Billy up and Billy smelled cigarette smoke. It made him sad, bringing back memories of his dad. Doctor Ethane gently laid Billy on a bale of hay and examined him. Unwrapping the dressing from around his head, the doctor looked at the wound.

"You done a mighty fine job on this, Maw," he said. "It's healing nicely. I'll leave you some ointment to put on it to make it heal faster. How do you feel, son?"

"I feel okay," Billy said, looking around the barn. The mule was lying down in the corner, sleeping.

That evening, Billy sat at the table with Maw and Elvis. The food was delicious. There were white acre peas, cornbread, pork chops, mashed potatoes, and sweet iced tea. After supper, Maw invited Billy into the living room where a fire was in the fireplace. She gave Billy a coloring book and some crayons. Elvis got on the floor with Billy, coloring the opposite page.

"Sure am glad the doc brung these here newspapers," Maw said. Billy noticed a stack on the floor next to her chair.

"Read us some stuff, Maw," Elvis said as he got more comfortable on the floor. "I like to hear about them murders."

Billy had noticed there was no TV.

Maw cackled as she started turning pages of the newspapers. Each paper was very small and was from the town of Buck Snort.

"Okay," said Maw, "here's one about a fugitive, wanted for murder. It says here: 'Police are looking for Kenny Sunders, age 43, from Nashville, Tennessee. He allegedly killed his wife, Rose...'"

Billy's ears refused to hear any more. He saw Maw's mouth moving, but couldn't hear what she was saying. He saw Elvis sit up, lean forward, hands on knees, eyes wide, listening. Billy's mind raced. He had to help his daddy. He had to find him and help him.

"Billy! Yo, Billy! You all right, boy?" Maw yelled.

"I'm okay," Billy said and tried to smile at Maw.

"I didn't have no bidness reading this to you and your virgin ears, anyway. Come on, boy, bed time for yer."

Billy took Maw's hand as she led him to the room he was sharing with Elvis. Elvis stayed on the floor and continued to color. He didn't seem to notice that Maw and Billy had left the room.

CHAPTER 9

"Elvis, wake up, boy. Yer haf ter go fetch the doc. Billy's burning up with a fever." Maw shook Elvis hard.

He finally rolled over. "Leave me be, Maw. I'm tard. I need to sleep."

"Wha ya got ter be tard for? Ya ain't done nuttin, ya lazy little shit. Git yer ass out the bed and go fetch the doc."

"It's ten miles to doc's house, Maw. It'll take the rest of the night to git there. Quit shaking me, Maw," he said as he swung his legs out of the bed.

"You best put some shoes on, Elvis. It's a might cold out thor. Ya might even need a jacket. Sorry ya haf to go on foot, Elvis, but ya know the mule's sick."

After Elvis left, Maw piled all the covers she had on top of Billy, to try to sweat him. She hoped the fever would break, if he got a good sweat going.

Billy moaned. "Don't hit me no more, Rose. Quit! I'll tell dad. Ow, that hurts. Please quit. I won't tell dad," he said. He began to cry, as he tried to throw the heavy covers off.

"Poor little tyke. This Rose person…
wait a minute."

Maw hurried to the living room and got
the paper she had been reading. *The woman
killed was named Rose. Of course it had to
be a coincidence. A lot of people were
named Rose. But what if it's her. If it is, then
Billy's dad is in deep shit. I got to find a way
to help Billy to find his dad.*

Billy felt like his head would explode.
He was so hot and wondered, in his
delusional state, if he was in hell. He had
heard an evangelist, on TV once, screaming
about hell and it had scared Billy. Tears
streamed down Billy's face. When Maw
bent over him with a wet cloth, Billy
thought it was Rose. He screamed.

Maw shushed him and said, "It's all
right, Billy. You're going to be all right."
She placed the cold cloth on his brow and
Billy became calm. The moisture felt so
good. Maw stayed with Billy, feeding him
liquids and mopping his head with cold
compresses, until morning. Finally, Elvis
arrived with the doctor.

"The head wound has become infected,"
the doctor said. "I'm going to have to open it

back up and clean it out. I'll give him a mild sedative."

Maw assisted the doctor, bringing fresh hot water and handing him things when he needed them. Billy slept through the whole ordeal. Around noon, Billy's fever broke and he felt like a new person. The first thing he thought about was finding his daddy. He was grateful to Maw, but he needed to get out of there. He decided to leave that night, while Maw and Elvis were asleep.

CHAPTER 10

Billy moved slowly down a hill, careful not to fall again. No longer having a backpack, he had tied food into a towel, put on his jacket and left the hillbilly shack. Still weak, but he was determined to find his dad. It was his fault that his dad was in trouble. He shouldn't have run away. If he hadn't run away, his dad wouldn't have been mad at Rose. Rose would still be alive. It would have been better for Billy to get hit by Rose, than for his daddy to be on the run. He should have waited until he was a big boy, before leaving home.

"How am I going to find my daddy?" Billy asked himself, wiping his eyes on his shirt sleeve.

In the early evening, Billy sat on a boulder and opened the towel. Taking out a piece of cornbread, he ate hungrily. He had wrapped up a big chunk of ham in tinfoil and a big piece of pound cake. He would need to find some water soon.

When it began to get dark, Billy became frightened. He should have taken a flashlight. His had been in the backpack, now lost somewhere on the hill in back of

Maw's house. He had never slept out in the open, without his tent. How was he going to survive in the woods, all alone, with nothing but cornbread, cake and ham?

Afraid of falling once again, Billy sat down and leaned against a tree. His head was beginning to throb with a dull ache. He dozed on and off, awaking every time he heard a sound. He was so tired. He missed his daddy. He even missed Maw and Elvis. When the sun began to warm his face, Billy realized that he had slept deeply. He got up and stretched. Grabbing his few belongings, he headed toward the sun. His daddy had taught him that the sun rose in the east. Since he wanted to go southeast, he would keep going straight ahead for awhile and then go to the right for awhile.

He walked all day, every day, until he could no longer see. He then slept until the sun came up. The food didn't last and he was weak and starving. Looking into the many trees, he wondered how the leaves would taste.

One day, he came to a campground and circled around it. Waiting until nightfall, he made his way to a trash can near the edge of the camp and rummaged through it. There were three small fish and two hushpuppies wrapped in tinfoil. He folded the foil back up and stuck the package inside his jacket. There was part of a banana, still in the peel. Billy broke off the part where someone had bit it and ate the rest while standing there. Nothing had ever tasted so good. He saw a flashlight coming toward him and backed away, making as little noise as possible. Whoever was behind the flashlight turned before reaching the can where he had been and was soon out of sight. Deciding not press his luck by continuing to look through the garbage, he headed off down another hill.

He rationed the fish and hushpuppies for several days, only allowing himself one small portion each day. When that ran out, all he could think about was food. He began to have a hard time sleeping with his stomach empty. He was weak, tired and discouraged. Once he cried himself to sleep and woke up to the feel of someone's hand against his cheek, but when he opened his eyes, there was no one there. Afraid that he was losing his mind, Billy trudged on. *It sure is a long way to Florida!*

Almost to the point of giving up, lying down and sleeping forever, he came across several trees of cherries. The trees were very colorful, the cherries in varieties of green, red, purple and black. This was the Wild Black Cherry. But Billy didn't know that. He thought the red ones were the ripe ones and the black ones were rotten. He ate the red ones even though they were very sour, filling his little belly until it swelled. He now had more energy and continued down another hill. Not even an hour later, he felt cramps like he had never experienced before. He soon had to squat down and lose all the cherries he had eaten. Then he was weaker than ever. Barely able to walk, he still pressed on, only thinking of his daddy.

Without realizing it, Billy had cut across the southwest corner of North Carolina, across the tip of Georgia and into South Carolina. If Billy had known he had crossed so many states in such a short period of time, he wouldn't have been surprised. He was good at geography, and knew that a corner of each of those states came together in such a way so that you could cross all of them in a short period of time. It was getting warmer, but he still needed his jacket. The land was becoming flatter.

Billy walked for several more days after eating the cherries. He was in a small town, Monroe Beach, Georgia. Billy had never seen the ocean before and thought it was beautiful. Spotting a hot dog stand, his stomach growled.

Standing on the beach, watching people get hot dogs, Billy wanted to see if anyone didn't finish theirs. A young mother handed her little boy a hot dog and he ate hungrily. Billy wished he had a mama to buy him a hot dog. He suddenly felt so lonely, he thought he would die.

A group of teenagers, three girls and two boys, laughed and talked as they ordered corndogs, French fries and Pepsi. While the attendant was busy filling their order, Billy snuck over to the corner of the stand and grabbed a handful of ketchup, mustard, and mayonnaise packets, stuffing them into his pockets. When he turned around he almost ran into a young couple. The man had on a sheriff's uniform.

The uniform scared Billy and he took off down the beach. Robert Kola, Sheriff of Monroe Beach, stared after Billy.

"Wonder what's going on with that kid," he said. "He looked scared to death."

His wife, Sarah, looked to where he was pointing. "Do you think he's a run-away, Robert?"

"He might be. He's gone over one of the sand dunes. Get me a corn dog. I'm going to talk to him."

"Let me, honey. Your uniform might have been what scared him off. I think I'll take him a corn dog."

When their order was ready, Sarah grabbed the corn dog and ran toward the dune she had seen the kid disappear behind.

Robert watched as his wife ran toward where the boy had disappeared. She was five months pregnant. He was worried about her. They had lost her last baby and they had almost split up over it. He wanted her to slow down but she insisted on exercising strenuously. Robert knew not to interfere. It had been the trouble before.

Sarah walked over the sand dune and there he was, opening packets of condiments and sucking out the contents greedily. He looked like he was starving to death. He had his back to her and didn't see her come up.

Billy jumped when he heard her say, "You want a corn dog?"

She held it out toward him, waiting for him to make up his mind.

He looked at her and then looked around as if looking for an escape route. She smiled at him and his heart melted. She looked so kind, as she held out the corn dog to him. Billy wanted it so badly, he was so hungry, but this lady's husband was the sheriff. Billy had to make up a story so that the sheriff wouldn't know who he was. If he found out who Billy was, then he might figure out who his daddy was, and he might join in the search for him.

Billy took the corn dog and, as they walked toward the stand, she said, "My name's Sarah, what's yours?"

"Billy."

Sarah wanted to ask him where his parents were, if he lived around there, and what he was doing alone on the beach, but she didn't want to scare him off.

Robert watched Sarah and the boy come across the beach. Sarah was good with kids; he thought she was going to make a wonderful mother.

Robert's cell phone rang and he dropped his corndog as he reached for it. "Damn! Sheriff Kola, here," he said. "Dr. McCain! How are you? Sarah and I were just talking about you a while ago. When you coming to see us? We haven't seen you in, what, four years? You're kidding! Don't rent a car. I'll pick you up."

Robert disconnected just as Sarah and the boy got to where he was standing. He smiled down at the boy, and said "Hi," and then turned to Sarah. "You're not going to believe this, Sarah. That was Judith on the phone. She and Wade just got married and are getting ready to land in Savannah. They're going to spend part of their honeymoon here in Monroe Beach. I told them not to rent a car. I'm going to pick them up."

Robert kissed Sarah on the cheek and hurried off. Billy breathed a sigh of relief. Sarah was glad Robert was called away for awhile, so that she could spend some time getting to know Billy. She was also looking forward to seeing Judith and Wade again.

Bending down eye level with Billy, Sarah asked, "Would you like another corn dog or would you rather have a hot dog, Billy?"

Billy had a hard time making up his mind. He thought the hot dog would fill him up more, but the corndogs looked so good.

Sensing his hesitation, Sarah said, "How about one of each, and some French fries."

He nodded, too excited to speak.

"What do you want to drink?"

"I'd like a Pepsi, please."

Sarah got herself a corndog and a cup of coffee. Handing Billy the paper bag filled with his order, she led him to a sand dune. They sat watching the waves in the ocean while they ate. Neither one said anything. Sarah was trying to think of a way to question Billy without being threatening. Billy was trying to decide whether or not he could trust Sarah enough to tell her about his daddy. He wondered if he could make her promise not to tell the sheriff. He had no idea how to find his daddy and wondered if Sarah could help him.

CHAPTER 11

Billy and Sarah walked on the beach for
hours, talking, after they finished eating.
Sarah had found out Billy was eight years
old, was from Tennessee, his mother was
dead, and he liked to fish and camp out with
his daddy. She didn't ask him why he had
run away from home. Sarah hoped he would
eventually trust her enough to open up more.

She took him to her upscale beachwear
boutique. A teenage girl was inside, hanging
up bikinis. She smiled when she saw Sarah.

"Sarah, these new swim suits just came
in. Aren't they gorgeous? I'm going to buy
this lime green one," said the teenager.

As Sarah and the girl talked business,
Billy walked around looking. He picked up a
sweatshirt that said Monroe Beach. It was
light blue, his favorite color. The shirt was a
woman's size extra small. Billy held it up to
him.

"I think it'll fit you, Billy. Why don't
you try it on?" Sarah said, causing Billy to
jump.

He folded the shirt and returned it to the pile of sweatshirts on the table.

"No," he said with regret, "I don't need it."

"We're friends, aren't we, Billy?' Sarah asked. Without waiting for a reply, she handed the shirt to him. "I can give a friend a gift, can't I?"

Billy only hesitated for a second before taking the shirt. "Thank you, Ma'am," he said. He took off his jacket and pulled the shirt over his head. It came to just above his knees and the sleeves were too long. Sarah knelt down and rolled up the sleeves.

"It will shrink some, after it's washed, and then it will fit better, Billy. This is a good color for you. It goes with your brown and dark brown hair."

Billy loved the shirt and loved Sarah. He didn't think she would ever hit him. He wished Sarah was his mama. As they walked out of the store, Billy suddenly started missing Maw. She had been kind to him. In some ways, Billy wished he had stayed with her and Elvis, but he had to find his dad.

"…and so, I'd like to take you and show you my condo," Sarah was saying.

"Okay," Billy said as he took her hand.

Not far down the beach from the boutique was a condo complex. Sarah unlocked a side door of one of the units that led into a garage. They walked up a flight of stairs and Sarah opened another door that led into a foyer.

"This is my condo, Billy. I bought it before I married Robert. We now live in a house in town. I miss living on the beach, but this condo is too small for two people, especially if one of them is as big as Robert. I thought I would let Judith and Wade stay here if they want to. They're a couple we know who just got married and are coming to Monroe Beach for their honeymoon. That's where Robert went, to pick them up at the airport in Savannah."

Billy walked around, looking. He wondered what it would be like to live in a condo like this, right on the beach. Walking over to the big window facing the ocean, he thought he could watch the waves all day long. No two were alike.

"Billy," Sarah called from the bedroom. "You want to come help me a minute?"

Reluctantly leaving the view, he found Sarah in the bedroom, stripping the bed.

"These sheets are clean, but I'm going to wash them and put some fabric softener in the rinse cycle to make them smell good."

Billy helped her strip the bed while continuing to look out at the ocean from the bedroom window. The ocean had a hypnotic affect on him. When they finished, Sarah handed Billy a feather duster.

"You want to dust some for me, Billy, while I take these down to the laundry room?"

Billy ran the duster over every surface. When Sarah came back, he was finished.

"Would you like some sweet iced tea, Billy?" Sarah asked. "I keep some here so that when I run on the beach I can stop by and have some."

Without waiting for Billy to reply, she got two tall glasses down from the cabinet, filling them with ice and tea.

"Here you go, Billy," she said, handing him one of the glasses. "Let's sit on the balcony and watch the waves."

Sarah smiled as she watched Billy, while he watched the ocean. It was almost as if he forgot where he was. His glass of tea was setting on the tiny table between them, untouched. She thought now would be a good time to get him to talk.

"What's your last name, Billy?"

"Sunders," Billy said, and then clamped his hand over his mouth.

She felt sorry that she had asked. He looked terrified. She decided to back off. Maybe between Robert, Judith and Wade they could find out about Billy from the last name.

Changing the subject, Sarah said, "The couple, who Robert is picking up from the airport is Dr. Judith McCain and Wade Russell. Dr. Judith is a psychologist. They both work for the FBI. As soon as she said it, Sarah knew she shouldn't have mentioned the FBI."

Billy picked up his tea and drank it all down while his eyes shifted everywhere. He set the glass down and said, "Thanks for the hot dogs and tea, but I need to be going, now."

He stood up and started for the door. Sarah followed him.

"Can't you stay with us for awhile, meet Judith and Wade, and get to know us all before you continue on your journey? We'd be glad to have you stay with us for a few days. How about it, Billy? Stay here awhile."

Billy looked down at his feet while standing on first one foot and then the other. "Nah, I really got to be going."

Sarah decided to go for broke, since she had already blown it anyway. "Where are your parents, Billy?"

"I need to use the rest room," Billy said.

"Oh, okay. It's right through there."

Locking the door to the restroom, Billy went to the window and looked out. He was small enough to fit, but they were on the second floor. He wondered if he could jump. There was nothing but a pile of sand below. It looked soft. Billy raised the window and then flushed the commode. Turning on the water, he left it running while he climbed out the window. Jumping, he tucked in and rolled, just like he had seen paratroopers do on TV. And then he ran.

Running away from the beach, Billy headed inland. He crossed the same bridge he had come across coming into Monroe Beach, and headed for the woods. Turning to the left, Billy headed south. He slowed down and walked until dusk. As the sun dropped below the horizon, Billy spotted a cabin. Crouching down, he peaked into the window.

Billy's jaw dropped at what he saw.

CHAPTER 12

Sarah was in the kitchen having a cup of tea when Robert came in.

"I'm in the kitchen, honey," she called out when she heard the screen door slam.

"Where's the boy?" Robert asked as he came in looking around.

"He ran away. Did you take Judith and Wade to the condo?"

"What do you mean he ran away? I thought you were keeping an eye on him."

Sarah inhaled deeply and let her breath out in one long sigh. "I took him to the condo; he helped me get it ready for Judith and Wade. We had tea on the balcony and then he said he had to go to the bathroom. He jumped out the window and ran, Robert. I made a mistake. I told him that Judith and Wade were with the FBI. He had said he had to leave and I was trying to get him interested in staying. I thought he might like to meet some FBI agents, but it was a mistake. I'm worried about him. His name's Billy Sunders, by the way. I did get that much from him."

"Sunders?" Robert ran his hands over his face as if washing without water. "Why does that name sound familiar? It's not a common name." He then shrugged. "Well it'll come to me. In the meantime I'm calling Freddy to tell him to put out an amber alert," he said while taking his cell phone out of his shirt pocket.

Sarah watched Robert make the call to his deputy. She hoped they could find Billy.

"His name's Billy Sunders, about eight or nine years, blond, blue. You too? Oh, yeah, that's right. I remember now. Well I'll be damned. Might be his dad. Well, keep me posted."

When Robert disconnected he turned to Sarah. "I knew I had heard that name before. We got a bulletin just a couple of days ago. There's an arrest warrant out for a Kenneth Sunders. He's wanted for killing his wife, Rose."

"Oh, Robert y'all have to find Billy and help him. His dad may be a murderer. Billy might be running from him."

"Don't worry, honey. We'll find him." He looked at his watch. "We're going to meet Judith and Wade for dinner. How soon can you be ready?"

Robert and Sarah had met Dr. Judith McCain twenty one years before. She had been called to Monroe Beach when a psychopathic killer, who called himself *Twoon,* was terrorizing people on the beach. Sarah had been a suspect. It had been Judith's job to do a psychological evaluation on Sarah.

They had met Wade Russell a few years later when he and Judith had been assigned to Monroe Beach on another case. Wade had worked for the Houston police department, but had joined the FBI before coming to Monroe Beach. The four had become good friends, and had kept in touch, but it had been a long time since they had seen each other.

Judith and Wade were standing outside the restaurant when Robert and Sarah pulled up. Sarah was amazed at how little Judith had aged. The car had barely come to a stop before Sarah opened the door and ran to greet the couple. After hugs all around, Judith held Sarah away from her.

"You look fantastic, Sarah," Judith said. "How are you feeling?"

"I'm fine, but you're the one who looks great. Don't you ever age?"

Just then Robert walked up. "Let's get a table. There's something we need to talk to y'all about."

They ordered the house special which was prime rib, baked potato and salad. Wade picked out a bottle of red wine. While they waited for their order, Robert explained about Billy.

When he finished, Judith said, "I never told y'all this, but I was a run-away when I was fifteen years old. It was very frightening experience. Billy sound like he's street smart, but he's got to be scared out of his wits. If this Kenneth Sunders is his dad, then Billy probably feels as if he's caught in the middle. He probably doesn't know who he can trust. He may have run away from his daddy, but my guess is that he also wants to protect his daddy."

"So, how can we help you guys?" Wade asked.

They paused while the waiter delivered their food. Then Robert said, "You're on your honeymoon, but if you could take a few minutes to go into your database and see if you have any information on Kenneth Sunders and their family dynamics."

Wade nodded as he tasted his prime rib. "This is the best prime rib I've ever tasted." He swallowed, took a sip of wine and said, "We'll get right on that as soon as we finish this delicious meal."

CHAPTER 13

There was a fire in the fireplace. A pot of stew was simmering on the stove and pot of coffee was dripping. Sitting in a rocking chair, in front of the fire, was a man crying. It was Kenny Sunders, Billy's daddy.

Tears of joy streamed down Billy's face, but he was scared too. His daddy was in trouble, and he had to help him, but he didn't know how. After all, Billy was only eight years old. He went to the front door and tried to open it. It was locked. The light inside went out.

"Open the door, Daddy. It's Billy."

The light came back on and Kenny picked Billy up, carrying him inside. They hugged for a long time, both crying. When he put Billy down, Kenny said, "Son, where have you been? We looked all over for you. We had a search party out there for three days."

"I'm sorry, Daddy. I had to leave. Rose kept hitting me and I was afraid to tell you. I thought you loved her."

"Well, Rose had been taken care of. Now I'm on the run."

"I know, Daddy. I know." Billy told Kenny about falling off the mountain, ending up in a hillbilly shack with Maw and Elvis, about the horse doctor who patched him up, and about the stack of newspapers the vet had left for Maw.

"Elvis wanted Maw to read to him. I don't think he could read. He's kind of simple. She read about you killing Rose and about the police looking for you. I knew I had to find you and help you, Daddy. But I didn't know where to look. I was on my way to Florida and ended up here, in Monroe Beach.

"I met the sheriff and his wife, Sarah. He had to leave, but she bought me a hot dog and took me to her condo. When she started asking me about my parents, I ran. I been running through these woods and saw this cabin and looked in. I can't believe I found you."

Billy stopped talking and looked around the cabin. There was only one room with a kitchenette, and a bunk bed shoved against the wall. The place was clean and there were braided rugs on the floor.

"Whose cabin is this, Daddy?"

"I don't know, I ditched my truck when I got into Georgia and hiked back in here. The key to the front door was under the welcome mat. I let myself in, found some food and coffee and started cooking. You hungry, boy?"

"I'm starving, Daddy. Is the food ready?"

Kenny walked over to the stove and lifted the lid on the pot of stew. Taking a spoon, he tasted it.

"Looks ready to me. See if you can find some bowls while I pour us a cup of coffee. I saw some cups over here somewhere."

The stew was delicious and Billy had two bowls. While Billy ate, Kenny studied him, deep in thought. After they had eaten, Billy yawned, eyeing the beds.

"I'll take the top bunk, Daddy," Billy said as he took of his jeans and sweatshirt.

After tucking his son in, Kenny sat thinking. He couldn't take Billy with him. *Maybe it would be better for the boy to stay right here in Monroe Beach. Maybe the nice lady, Sarah and her husband would take care of him. If I don't tell Billy where I'm going, then he can't tell the sheriff.*

Kenny sat up all night, smoking and drinking coffee. As the sky was getting pink, he decided to sneak out and leave Billy there. He found a pen and paper in the drawer of a small table next to the bunk beds. He was standing there sucking on the end of the pen, trying to think what to write, when Billy rolled over and looked at his daddy.

"What are you doing, Daddy? You going to write a letter or something?"

Kenny jumped and looked at his son. He was going to have to break his heart and it was killing him.

"Come on down here, son. I need to talk to you."

Billy jumped down, without climbing the ladder and put on his jeans and sweatshirt. Reaching into his pocket, Kenny pulled out his wallet and counted out a hundred dollars. Billy looked fearful as he gazed down at the money in his hand. He thought he knew what his daddy was going to say. He shoved the money back.

"I don't need any money, Daddy. I don't want to stay with anyone but you. Please, Daddy, please."

It broke Kenny's heart, but he couldn't take Billy with him. It wouldn't be fair to him. He wished he had a brother or sister to leave him with, but he had no one. He could see he was going to have to be tough.

"I don't want you with me, Billy. I can't afford to feed you. It costs too much."

"I won't eat much, Daddy. Please, Daddy. I want to go with you."

"Let go of my arm, Billy," Kenny said as he pushed him away and headed for the door.

Billy lay down on the floor and cried. His heart was broken. He was all alone. *No one wants me. No one cares what happens to me. I'm so scared.* He cried himself to sleep. When he awoke, it was dark outside and he helped himself to the last of the stew. Crawling under the covers in the lower bunk, he sniffed the smells of his daddy and, once again, cried himself to sleep.

CHAPTER 14

Judith woke up the next morning smelling bacon and coffee. She stretched and looked out the window, at the ocean. She was so glad she had finally married Wade. It had taken a long time to get over the death of Ben, but she knew she and Wade would have a good life together.

Wade came in carrying a tray loaded with food. "Good morning, sleepy head," he said, putting the tray on the dresser.

They stacked pillows against the headboard, and then Wade laid the tray between them.

"I could get used to this," Judith said, as she took a cup of coffee and a piece of bacon. "Are you always going to do this, or just on our honeymoon?"

Wade took a big bite out of a piece of toast and winked at her. Then taking a swallow of coffee, he said, "I was going to say that you could bring me breakfast in bed sometimes too, but I don't want to wait until noon to have breakfast."

She slapped him playfully on the arm. "I've never been a morning person, but I do not sleep until noon."

"Ow," Wade said, laughing. "By the way, I'm glad I brought my laptop. I interfaced with the police database in Nashville, where they're from, and found out quite a bit about Billy's family. Apparently, over the last three years, the police were called out on domestic abuse calls a total of forty six times. They lived in a trailer park and the neighbors called about the disturbances.

"When the police arrived, both husband and wife looked like they had been beaten. Neither one would press charges. My guess is that Kenneth Sunders finally snapped and killed his wife, Rose."

"Do you want more coffee, Wade? If not I'm going to finish the pot. I sure hope they find that little boy. I was lucky when I ran away. I could have been killed."

"Well, you were almost raped. I'm glad you found the people who helped you. You've done well for yourself, Judith."

"Thanks honey. By the way, if you want to hang out with Robert and them, I'm dying to see what Sarah has in her shop. I know you're not going to let a little ole thing like a honeymoon get in your way of doing some man things."

Wade stood up, taking the tray off the bed. "Well, I didn't expect to be joined at the hip for the whole trip. So, yeah, let's meet up for supper," he said, taking the tray into the kitchen. When he came back, Judith was in the shower. Wade took off his shorts and joined her. As he was getting in, he said, "You need your back washed?"

When Wade got to the sheriff's office, he found a meeting going on in the conference room. Robert saw him and motioned for him to come in. Most of the deputies remembered Wade from when he came to Monroe Beach to help solve the case involving the serial killer who raped women and then baptized them, holding their heads under water until they were dead.

"We think we have a sighting on Kenneth Sunders, Wade. You remember my fishing cabin I took you to last time you were here?"

Wade nodded and Robert continued, "I got a call this morning from my nearest neighbor. He was driving by, last night, on the way to town, and saw a light on in my cabin. He said there was a man sitting in there in front of the fireplace. From his description, it sounds like Sunders. I'm just fixing to head on out there. You want to come along?"

"Wouldn't miss it for the world."

"I guess the girls have gone shopping," Robert said as he backed out.

"Yeah, Judith wanted to see what Sarah has in her shop, and then I guess they'll go into Savannah and make a day of it. I'll tell you, Judith is getting as bad as her grandmother, about shopping."

"I'll always be grateful to Judith for the help she gave Sarah, back when Sarah had four personalities. If it hadn't been for Judith and Dr. Anna, no telling what would have happened to her. We sure were sorry to lose Dr. Anna."

Wade nodded. "I never met the woman, but from what I've heard, she could work miracles. Both Judith and her twin sister, Julia were able to heal their childhood issues with Dr. Anna's help."

Robert slowed the car and pulled into a narrow dirt road. The cabin was just a few yards in. Robert cut the engine and let the car coast to a stop. They got out and left the doors ajar.

"I'll take the rear," Wade said, taking his gun out of his shoulder holster.

They crouched and ran from tree to tree, and then Wade veered off and headed for the back. He tried the back door. It was unlocked. The front door opened just as easily for Robert. The two men stood looking around. Kenneth Sunders wasn't there, but Billy was sound asleep, curled up on the bottom bunk.

"Looks like he was here," Wade whispered, holding up two bowls coated with stew.

"Yeah, and they helped themselves to my stew and coffee."

They stood studying Billy for a few moments and then Robert gently shook his shoulder. "Billy, wake up, son. We need to talk to you."

Billy thought his dad had come back for him, but when he opened his eyes and saw the big black sheriff, he jumped up and ran.

Wade was waiting at the door and scooped Billy up, holding him gently.

"Whoa, little fellow," Wade said, laughing. "Calm down, we're not the enemy."

"Put me down," Billy cried.

"You promise not to run if I put you down?"

Billy wiped his nose on his sleeve. "I won't run."

Wade put Billy in a straight back chair and squatted down in front of him while Robert leaned against the wall and watched.

"My name's Wade. That's a nice sweat shirt, Billy."

"I didn't steal it. Sarah gave it to me. She's my friend."

Robert spoke up, "She's worried about you, Billy. She thought you were going to stay with us for awhile. You're not in any trouble, son. We all want to be your friends. What do you say? Why don't you come on back into town with us and stay a few days. We'd be glad to have you."

They waited while Billy sat there thinking. *Do they really just want to be my friend or are they being nice to try and find*

Daddy. I can't tell them where he is. I don't know where he went. I would like to see Sarah again. She was nice to me. I could stay a little while and rest up and then head on down to Florida.

Billy nodded. He had made up his mind. "Okay, I'll go with you."

"Wonderful," Robert said and Wade nodded his approval.

Billy sat between the two men on the way back into town. He couldn't believe he had run so far. It took quite awhile to get back to Monroe Beach in the car.

"You walked a long way, Billy," Wade said as if he had read his mind. "You want to have lunch with us?"

Billy looked at the sheriff who winked at him. Billy smiled. *Maybe it won't be so bad.*

CHAPTER 15

Judith and Sarah sat on the balcony of the condo, watching the waves and catching up with each other's lives.

"I'm so happy for you, Sarah. Do you know whether it's a boy or a girl?"

Sarah laughed. "It's a girl. Guess what we're going to name her?"

Judith shrugged. "Josephine?"

"What? Where did that come up?"

"It just came out."

Sarah took a sip of iced tea. "We're going to name her Judith, but we're calling her Judy."

Judith got up and gave Sarah a big hug. "I feel honored. Thank you."

"I'm sorry you can't have any children, Judith. But you will always be Judy's aunt."

Judith's cell phone rang. "Hello, darling. You found Billy?" She looked at Sarah and gave a thumb up.

Sarah walked to the other end of the balcony to give them some privacy. Judith disconnected almost immediately and started punching in numbers.

Sarah heard her say, "This is Dr. Judith McCain. Is her honor in?"

Winking at Sarah, she motioned her to come closer. Judith put her hand over the mouthpiece. "Wade wanted me to call this judge I became friends with during the Jupiter Case, in New Orleans. Her name is Judge June Meadows. She's black, wears a size two and makes Judge Judy look like a pussy cat. Hopefully, she can give me a name for a judge here so that we can get a temporary custody order for Billy. We don't want him to end up in the foster care system. I was in that most of my childhood and I hated it."

Sarah started to comment, but Judith held up her finger. Sarah listened to her side of the conversation.

"It's good to hear your voice too, Judge. Well, thank you. It was horrible losing Ben. It's taken a long time to get over it, but at least we took another psychopath off the streets. I just got married. Why, thank you. We're in Monroe Beach for our honeymoon.

"You did? Did you change your name? No, I didn't either. Congratulations. No honeymoon? Oh, okay. The reason I'm calling is we have a kid here, a run-away, who we want to get temporary custody of. There has been an Amber Alert out for him, but that was before his daddy killed his step-mom. Yep, that's the one.

"Do you know any judges in this area you could recommend to help us?" She listen a while and then said, "Thank you so much, Judge. Goodbye.".

"I have to go see a judge, Sarah," Judith said. "Judge Meadows is calling a Judge Hemmings. She said we could go pick up the court order from him. You want to come with me?"

CHAPTER 16

Before she joined the FBI, Judith McCain had been a psychologist in private practice. Although she never had children of her own, she loved working with them. When she met Billy, she could tell right away that he had been abused. He was overly polite, seeming to weigh each word before speaking, as if he was afraid of being punished if he said the wrong thing. She had met so many kids like that. Her heart went out to him.

Billy sat between Sarah and Judith at the Crab Shack, a new restaurant on the beach. He had never eaten crab before. They were teaching him how to crack them, while Robert and Wade sat at the bar drinking beer.

"This was a good idea, Robert, giving the three of them time together. I think, between Judith and Sarah, Billy might open up about his daddy," Wade said.

They watched as Billy tried to open a crab. They were laughing and having a good time.

Robert took a big swallow of beer and set the glass down on the bar with a loud bang. "At this point, I'd rather help Billy than look for his daddy. You're the FBI. His daddy has already crossed state lines, so you can go for it. But, for now, I want to protect the boy. You can tell he's been through some hard times. Don't try to get information from him, Wade."

"No, I agree with you, Robert. Besides, Judith and I are on our honeymoon. I intend to enjoy every minute of it. It took Judith a long time to agree to marry me. By the way, we were able to get a temporary custody order for Billy. It's just for ten days, but it gives us some time with him."

Robert nodded his head. "So, how long did y'all take off work?"

"Three weeks. We were planning to spend one week here and then heading on down the coast of Florida, all the way to the Keys. I've never been, have you?"

"No, Sarah and I have always wanted to go down there and catch some lobster."

"The waters are too warm for lobster, aren't they?"

"Well, actually what they call Florida Lobster is really giant crawfish. But you won't be able to tell the difference."

"Hum, I never knew that," Wade said. "That's very interesting. Hey, why don't we all go? Can you take some time off?"

Robert rubbed his chin. "I could, and Sarah could close her shop, but are you sure you want us to tag along on your honeymoon?"

"Hell, I think it's a wonderful idea. I think Billy will love it." Wade picked up his beer and headed over to the table. "Hey, Judith, how do you feel about everyone, including Billy, going down to the Keys?"

Billy was so excited. "Can I really go with y'all?'

"You betcha, son," Robert said. "Can you close your shop, Sarah?"

Sarah hugged Billy. "I'll leave Sandy in charge. She can handle it."

CHAPTER 17

They got up early the next morning and packed Robert's Dodge Caravan. There was plenty of room for all five of them. Billy rode in the back by himself; Judith and Wade rode in the middle. Billy's eyes were as big as saucers as he watched the landscape go by.

"I hope y'all are okay with me taking US 1 most of the way down," Robert said as he turned onto the highway. "I don't like driving the freeways. It's boring."

Wade grinned from ear to ear. "Hey, it works for us! Judith and I always take the back roads. You see more that way."

They had started out before the sun rose, and were in St. Augustine in time for lunch. Driving over The Bridge of Lions, Robert pulled into the parking lot of Osteen's Restaurant.

Killing the motor, he turned in his seat. "I looked on the Internet before we left home and found this place. It had more five star reviews than any of the others."

They ordered three variety trays so that everyone could sample each dish. The food was delicious. When Billy was asked what he liked the best, he said he liked the crab cakes. Sarah put all the crab cakes on his plate.

Later, as they were getting into the van, Robert said, "I'm going to take the coastal route. It's about eight and a half hours from here to Key West, according to Map Quest. It's now 1:10 P.M. Do y'all want to drive all the way to Key West tonight, or maybe stop in Miami and spend the night?"

"I'd rather spend the night in Miami," Wade said. "If we drive straight through, then we won't be able to see all the views from the bridges I keep hearing about."

"Why don't we drive to the first key?" Sarah said.

Robert smiled at her. "Ah, can't wait to see the island from your favorite movie, huh."

"Key Largo, starring Humphrey Bogart and Lauren Bacall," Judith said from the middle seat.

Without thinking, Billy shouted, "My dad loves that movie!"

No one said anything at first, then Judith spoke up, "I love it too, sweetie. Have you watched it with your daddy?"

"I did, but I didn't like it. It's a sissy movie."

Everyone was trying hard not to laugh, but Robert was unsuccessful. He roared with laughter. "I agree with you, Sport. I'll take a John Wayne movie any day."

Now that someone agreed with him, Billy became braver. "The mean man in the movie kept whispering to the nice lady, but they didn't let us know what he was saying. It was silly."

This time, everyone laughed and Billy joined in. "That was the silliest part. I liked the hurricane part, though. I'd like to see one someday."

Traffic became heavier as they neared Miami and Robert headed back to US 1 to make better time. Since they could no longer see the ocean, everyone started dozing, except Judith and Robert. She leaned over the seat and whispered, "Robert, I think Billy is beginning to trust us now."

"Yeah, I hope he has a good time on the trip. When we get back, we need to try to figure out what to do with him. I don't want to stick him in foster care. But that will be up to the courts. We can't continue to keep him out of school either. We have a lot to think about."

"Well, let's concentrate on having a good time with Billy." What Judith didn't tell Robert was that she had been thinking about talking to Wade about adopting him. They both love kids and she hadn't been able to have any. Anyway, it was too early to think about that.

CHAPTER 18

Billy only pretended to sleep. He had heard everything Dr. Judith and the sheriff said. Like most abused kids, he was hyper vigilant. Even when he slept, he slept lightly. Now he was fully awake and thinking. He was always thinking. He knew he couldn't stay with Robert and Sarah for long. They would eventually put him in foster care. A boy at his old school had been in foster care and hated it. It must be worst than living with a step-mom. *I'm only eight years old. How am I supposed to survive on my own? But if I stay with adults, I won't have a choice in anything. I wish I could find someone I could trust to take care of me.*

The car was slowing down and everyone was stretching and yawning. Billy pretended he was waking up.

"Coffee time," Robert said as he shut off the motor.

Wade got out and bent over, touching his toes. "You want me to drive awhile, Robert?"

"Yeah, that would be nice. You can get back on A1A if you want to."

Wade watched as Sarah and Judith walked with Billy inside the truck stop. Then slapping Robert on the back he said, "I'm sure glad y'all decided to come on this trip with us. I want some strong, hot coffee before I start driving."

When they got inside, they found the two women trying on sunglasses. Billy was trying on trucker caps.

"We're going to go ahead and get a table," Wade said as he hugged Judith. "I like the green sunglasses, by the way."

As they walked away, Sarah called after them, "Order us some coffee. What would you like, Billy. Billy?"

"Well, he was right here," Judith said. She put the sunglasses back on the rack and walked around the corner of the counter. "Billy," she called louder.

Sarah started off in the opposite direction, calling his name. Then she ran to the dining area and found Robert and Wade. Seeing the alarm on her face, they stood.

"What's wrong, Sarah?" Robert asked.

"We can't find Billy. He was right next to us and all of a sudden he was gone."

Wade ran to the parking lot, looking into the cabs of the trucks. Robert ran to the men's room and looked in the stalls. Finding a back door that led to an alley, he ran outside and down the alley, calling Billy's name. Running back inside, he saw the other three adults standing in the aisle talking.

"Looks like he's run again," Wade said. "Damn! He could have gotten into any of the eighteen wheelers leaving just now. Did you call it in, Robert or should I?"

"I just sent out another Amber Alert. I hope he's hiding out in one of the semis. I hope no one has grabbed him."

Wade snorted. "I doubt anyone could hold onto that kid for long. I think he's more than likely hiding out in one of the trucks that's already left. I hope they get some road blocks set up soon enough to find him."

"The poor kid," Judith said with tears in her eyes. "He must have heard us talking, Robert. He must have gotten scared and bolted.

Sarah started crying and Robert put his arms around her. "Don't worry, Honey. He's a tough kid. He'll be all right."

They all had tears in their eyes as they hugged each other.

"What do y'all want to do?" Robert said.

"I vote for continuing on down into the

CHAPTER 19

Billy had hidden behind the seat in a truck that was taking a load of cars to the Keys. He had covered himself up with a blanket he found in the space he was in. Trying not to move, he heard the door open and then slam shut.

The driver coughed, then said, "Miles t' go before I sleep." It was a woman's voice.

She started mumbling to herself. At first Billy couldn't make out what she was saying and then he heard, "…Have to git rid of the body somewhurs, soons I see a back road."

Suddenly, her radio squawked. "Amber Alert, eight-year-old Billy Sunders, brown hair, brown eyes, may have hidden in an eighteen wheeler. Look in your cabs. Call the sheriff's department immediately if you find him."

"Whu? Jest what I need, fer some brat t' be hiding in m' cab."

Billy was terrified. He apparently had hidden in the truck with a murderer. He was going to get killed for sure, he thought.

The driver continued to mumble. "Whut the hell is I going t' do with a kid. He more than likely heard me." Then, raising her voice, she said, "Hey, boy, you in here?"

She laughed, wheezing until she started coughing. When the coughing subsided, she lit a cigar. It nearly took Billy's breath away. He tried hard not to cough, but he was unsuccessful. After holding it in for what seemed like forever, he let out a loud cough.

"Holy sheet," The driver screamed as she swerved over the middle line.

Trying to keep the truck in her own lane, she came close to jack knifing. When she finally got control, she pulled off on the shoulder. Leaning over the back of the seat, she threw the blanket off and grabbed Billy by both arms, pulling him into the front.

He was so scared he had his eyes closed tight.

"Open ya eyes, boy. Open ya eyes and look et me."

When he opened his eyes, they became big as saucers. Maw had no teeth and looked like a hag, but this woman, even with a mouth full of even white teeth, was a sight to behold. The layer of fat on her belly formed an apron that flapped over the waist of her jeans. With her narrow shoulders and flat chest, she was shaped like a pear. She could have been anywhere from 35 to 65 years old.

She started laughing. "Will, er y' through staring? I knowed I ain't that purdy t' look at. Did ya hear whut I said before?"

Without a word, Billy shook his head.

"I don't believe ya," she said, studying him with her black eyes.

Then she became quiet and sat staring out the window. "Whut em I goin t' do wit this kid," she mumbled. "How old er ya, boy?"

"I'm eight. I'll be nine next Monday."

"Huh, eight, nine, eight, nine." She shook her head as if to clear it. "Do you know about the difference between boys and girls?"

Billy nodded.

"Do ya know whut rape is?"

He stared at her. "I think so."

"Wil, here's the way tis. I come home from a long haul and found my boyfriend raping my little girl. Whut would you do iffen you found someone raping your sister or your mother?"

94

"I don't have a sister or mother," Billy said.

She looked at him while running her fingers through her pitch black hair. It was cut like a man's. "Wil, I'll tell y' whut I done. I got m' shotgun and kilt him. I took little Annie to m' mama's and now I got to get rid of the body. Do ya understand, boy? By the way, whut's yore name? Mine's Machida. I go by Mack."

"I'm Billy. I don't blame you for killing the mean man. My stepmom used to hit me, too."

She peered at him and wiped a stray tear off his cheek. "That why y' run away?"

"Yes, ma'am. If you don't turn me in, I won't turn you in."

Putting her hand out, she said, "Y' got yourself a deal. Put on that thur seat belt. I need t' git back on the road and find a place to bury this varmint."

Mack soon took an exit on the other side of Homestead. Driving down a few miles, she pulled onto a blacktop road and then onto a sandy, deep rutted road. The dirt road didn't look like any cars had been on it in a long time. There were weeds growing almost waist high in the middle. Billy wondered how she knew about this road.

"It's a road I sometimes come down iff'n I needs to take a nap. There's not always a motel whur y' needs it."

She didn't bother to pull off the road, but stopped in the middle. Without saying a word, she jumped down from the cab and walked around back. Climbing up where the cars were, Billy watched her open the trunk of a green car near the back and pull out a rolled up rug. He had seen bodies hidden in rugs in movies and TV shows, but knew this was a real person that had been killed with a shotgun. He tried not to look, but it was like trying not to look at a car wreck when driving past.

Mack leaned the rug against the back of the car and closed the trunk. She then jumped to the ground and slid the package after her.

Laying the body down along the side of the road, she opened the cab and said, "Reach over back o' the seat thur and git the shovel."

Handing her the shovel, Billy hoped she wouldn't ask him to help. Without a glance, she grabbed the shovel and headed for the woods, leaving the rolled up rug lying by the road. It seemed like she was gone a long time and Billy was beginning to wonder if she had gotten snake bitten or something. She finally came back, soaking wet with sweat from digging a grave. She picked up the roll as if it weighed nothing and headed back into the woods.

Billy had started dozing when the door opened and Mack climbed in. "Lit's fine us a motil room. I needs to get cleaned up."

He was amazed at how easily she backed the big semi out of the dirt road. It wasn't long before they pulled into the parking lot of a row of cabins. They were painted different colors.

Parking in front of the office, Mack said, "You stay here, I'll be right back."

Later, getting back into the cab, Mack drove around to a pink cabin at the very back. All the other cabins seemed to be empty. The building was rustic with one room and a bath. There were full-sized beds in the room with a nightstand beside each one.

Dropping her duffle bag heavily on the tile floor, Mack said, "I'm on go ahead and shower first. You kin turn on the TV iffn you wants to."

Billy sat on the end of one of the beds and turned on the TV. It was an old heavy set and the reception was terrible. As he was flipping through channels, he saw a school picture of himself. It was on a screen behind a beautiful blonde woman. Turning up the sound, he caught the last of the broadcast.

"In case you are just joining us, this is a picture of eight year old Billy Sunders, who disappeared from a truck stop south of Miami on US 1. It is believed that he could be hiding out in one a semi trucks. If you have any information, please call the number on your screen."

Mack's hand suddenly appeared and turned the TV off. "You can go git your shower now, boy. I'm done."

She was a sight to behold, wearing a long white gown gathered at the neck. It looked similar to a choir robe. She turned down one of the beds and crawled under the covers, immediately falling asleep. Billy would have liked to have something to eat, but she started snoring as soon as her head hit the pillow.

The next morning, Mack said, "You stay here. I need t' drive into the Keys and deliver these trucks, drive back t' Miami t' git m' pickup, and then drive back down here to get you. I'll be back sometime tomorrow."

She pulled her wallet out of her back pocket and handed Billy two twenties. "There's a Burger King across t' street. Ya kin eat there. Here, take this here cap and wear it low when ya go out. Keep this door locked at all times and don't lock yorsef out. You'll be all right."

He nodded. "I'll be all right."

CHAPTER 20

"I done tol ya and tol ya. That tiny sneaker belongs t' my little girl, Annie. I gots t' git this here load o cars down t' the Keys."

Clive Cooper, Deputy Sheriff of Dade County, turned his head away from Mack and spit a stream of tobacco juice on the shoulder for the highway. Turning back toward her, he rubbed his beer belly. He then turned the shoe over and looked at the bottom. It looked well worn.

"Well, Ms. Ruskin, here is my problem. We got a little boy missing and believed to have hidden out in a truck like yours. Now we stop you at this road block and find a child's shoe in your cab. I ain't saying you're lying, but I'm going to need you to come with me while we check out your story. Because, to tell you the truth, this is the first sign of any kid having been in any truck. And we've had this road block set up since yesterday afternoon."

Mack knew it was no use arguing with the deputy. "Okay, I'll go wit ya, but whut's goin t' happen t' m' truck?"

"It'll be towed and put in our lot. We need to look it over."

Mack now started getting worried. *I don't think I got any blood on anything, but what if I did an they fine it? Whut's goin t' happen t' little Billy, iffen they keeps me?*

Mack was taken into the small town of Salt Cove, Florida and questioned for hours while the sheriff waited for her truck to be processed. She was allowed to call her mama, to check on Annie. Then they put her in a cell. They later brought her supper of beans and corn bread. Around midnight, she finally gave up on the hope of getting out anytime soon. She stretched out on the thin mattress and fell asleep.

CHAPTER 21

Billy liked being on his own now that he had a place to sleep and enough food to eat. He loved the food at Burger King. He could watch TV all he wanted. His dad had never let him watch much. He missed his daddy and wondered where he was. Seeing himself on the screen just about every time he turned on the news, it was kind of fun to be famous and pretended he was a famous movie star.

At first Billy was glad Mack was late getting back, but after the third day he got worried. *What if she doesn't come back? I can't stay here forever. That maid that keeps asking to clean the room is eventually going to insist on getting in here. I keep telling her that my mama isn't feeling well and she needs to rest, and not be disturbed. How long before she figures out that I'm by myself?*

When he got out of the shower, Billy heard the rain. He parted the heavy curtain and peeked out the window. It was coming down in sheets. He couldn't see two feet in front of his face. There was a loud popping sound and a big lightning bolt struck the ground in front of the window. At the same time something caught his eye. It was yellow and it was in front of his door. At first he thought it was a bundle of clothes that someone had left. He was momentarily blinded by the lightning and waited for his eyes to adjust. The bundle moved and he realized it was someone sitting in the doorway. They were wearing a yellow raincoat and had the hood pulled over their head.

He couldn't tell if it was male or female, but was pretty sure it was a child. *Should I open the door? What if it's a mean midget? Nah, why would a mean midget hide in my doorway? Whoever it is, they must be scared and cold. Maybe it's another run-away, like me.*

He parted the curtain again and peeked out. The person was shaking, as if crying. He didn't think about it any longer, but walked over to the door and opened it. She fell into the room, the hood of her raincoat coming off her head. Her hair was long, blonde and wet. She was a teenager.

First falling into the room and then coming off the floor in one motion, she then jumped to her feet. Her baby blue eyes were wild as she turned in a circle with her fist raised in front of her face.

When she noticed Billy, she let out a nervous sounding laugh, and said, "Are you here by yourself?"

Before he could answer, she ran for the bathroom and slammed the door. He heard the commode flush and then she came out drying her hair on a towel. She had taken off her raincoat and wore a thin pink tee shirt and black jeans. The raincoat hadn't been very effective in keeping her dry. Her clothes were wet. She wore no bra and Billy stared at her small breasts.

"You got anything to eat?" she asked, while looking around the room.

When she spotted his leftover burger and fries on the nightstand, she grabbed them, stuffing the food into her mouth so fast he thought she was going to choke. Wiping her mouth on the back of her hand, she walked around the room.

"You got anything else?" she asked.

He shook his head. She stopped pacing and really looked at him for the first time. "You here by yourself, Kid?"

"Yeah, but Mack will be back any minute." He couldn't meet her eyes as he said this. He didn't know if Mack was coming back.

"Well, Kid. I'll tell you what, why don't I crash here until he gets back."

"She."

"Huh?"

"Mack is a woman."

"Oh," she said around a yawn. "I'm beat. I need to get some sleep."

Without another word, she curled up on Mack's bed and went to sleep. Billy watched her for awhile and then peeked out around the curtain to see if there was any sign of Mack. The rain was letting up and the sun was trying to come out. A black pickup truck pulled in. He thought it was Mack, but a woman and little girl got out and went into the cabin next door. He was getting hungry again and thought about going across the street to Burger King. He wondered if he should wake up the teenager and see if she wanted something. He didn't know what he was supposed to do. She might get mad if he woke her up. Rose used to hit him if he disturbed her afternoon nap. He didn't know if he should leave the teenager in the room alone. He was afraid to turn on the TV. Rose could always sleep with the TV on, but his dad couldn't. He didn't want to make this person mad at him.

Suddenly she jumped up so fast that Billy almost screamed. She looked around the room, wild-eyed, as if she didn't know where she was.

When her eyes finally became focused, she said, "Oh, hi, Kid."

"My name's Billy."

"Put er there, Billy," she said putting out her hand.

"I'm Sam," she said while shaking his hand. "How did you come to be here all by yourself? What's your story?"

Feeling like he could trust her, he said, "I ran away from home, to get away from my step-mama. She was a step-mom from hell."

"Well, we have something in common, then. I ran away from home too. My mom died and I was left with my step-dad. He thought I was going to take my mom's place, if you know what I mean."

"Oh, yeah, he wanted you to do all the cooking and laundry."

Sam snorted. "Something like that."

"Where did you come from?" Billy asked.

"Miami. How about you?"

"Nashville, Tennessee."

"That's a long ways. You hitched all the way down here?"

"Nah, I hiked most of the way, until I got to Monroe Beach, Georgia. Then I met some folks who brought me down to Florida. I heard them talking about putting me in Foster care and, when we stopped at a truck stop, I hid in Mack's truck. She brought me here and left to deliver some cars in the Keys. She said she was coming back yesterday but she's not back yet."

Sam thought for a minute then said, "You got any money?"

"Mack left me some money for food. You want something to eat? I can go across the street and get some burgers."

She went to the window and opened the curtains. "It's quit raining," she said.

"Close the curtains," he said as he jumped up and ran toward the window.

"Oh, I'm sorry. I guess you got people looking for you. I doubt my step-dad will even report me missing. I think he would be scared to. I'll tell you what, why don't you give me some money and I'll go get our burgers."

Billy had kept the money Mack had given him separate from the hundred dollars from his dad. He pulled out the last twenty Mack had left and handed it to her. "I want a Whopper Junior, an order of fries and a large coke."

She put the money in her jeans pocket. "You got an extra shirt? I left in a hurry and don't have any other clothes. This tee shirt is thin and I'm kind of cold."

He handed her his new Monroe Beach sweatshirt and she pulled it on over her tee. It fit perfectly. He thought about giving it to her, but Sarah had given it to him and he loved Sarah.

When she came back with the food, they ate while watching TV. During a commercial, Billy turned to the news channel so Sam could see him. He was disappointed that it showed so little of him now. They eventually fell asleep, each with their own nightmares.

CHAPTER 22

"Okay, Ms. Ruskin. You're free to go now," the sheriff said as he opened the cell door.

Mack stretched and yawned. "Why don't ya turn around and gimme some privacy so's I kin pee," she said.

He shook his head. "You're free to go; you don't have to use the toilet in here. You can use the one down the hall. That way, you'll have plenty of privacy."

After she used the bathroom and they returned her belongings, she got in her truck and drove toward the Keys. She knew she would be delayed further in getting back to the cabin and Billy, but she had no way to call him. The cabin had been rustic and had no phone. She broke the speed limit getting down to the Keys, spending all day delivering the cars to various dealers. Coming back to Homestead, where her pickup was, she exchanged the vehicles and got back on the road. She had been worried about Billy and was looking forward to seeing him. While driving, she took her cell phone out and called her mama.

"Mama, how's Annie?"

"Glad ya called, Mack. She been havin nightmires. She wakes up screaming. Ya think I should take er t' one o' them psycholgist?"

"I don know, Mama. Whut ifffn she tells him whut I done? He might report it t' tha cops. I already been held three days. They thought I kidnapped a kid. I'll tell ya about it later. Let me talk t' Annie."

"Hey, Mama," Annie said when was passed the phone.

"Ya okay, Baby? I don know when I'll git back, so jest mind Granny. You be okay."

"I be okay," Annie said. "Bye, Mama."

"Let me talk t' Granny agin."

"Mama, don worry bout Annie. She'll outgrow the nightmires."

"Okay, honey. Don worry. We be okay."

Mack arrived at the motel at around 1:00 A.M. Parking the truck in front of the cabin; she stretched and bent over, touching her toes. She was very flexible, even though she was large. She had left the only key with Billy, so she had to knock. He came to the door rubbing his eyes.

"Glad ya all right, boy," Mack said, patting him on the head. "Sorry I had t' wake ya. Go on back t' bed. I aim t' git some sleep m'self. Didn't sleep much the last few nights, but I needs a shower."

Although he was glad Mack was back, he was sleepy. He crawled back into bed, forgetting that Sam was in the other.

Mack came out of the bathroom and made her way toward her bed in the dark. She didn't want to wake Billy. Stubbing her toe on the corner of the bed, she stifled a curse. Sam came up out of the bed with fists raised. Mack saw only a shadow. She jumped back with a loud yawl. Billy jumped up and turned on the lamp by his bed. Everyone froze: Mack, with her mouth wide open; Sam, with fist raised and fire in her eyes; and Billy, with his hand over his mouth.

Then, everyone started talking at once:
Billy: I'm sorry, I should have…
Mack: Whut the fook!
Sam: Get away from me, you son of a …
The kids stopped and looked at Mack, waiting for the adult to make the decisions about this odd situation.

112

She looked at Billy. "Whut's goin on here. Boy? Who's this little spitfire?"

"She's a runaway, like me. I couldn't leave her in the cold. I mean, look at her; she's not much bigger than me. Her mama died and her step-dad was going to make her do all the cooking and cleaning."

"How old are ya, girl?"

"I'm 13 and can speak for myself. I'm Sam. Where did you learn to talk, anyway? Are you Mack? Billy told me all about you. You don't look anything like I pictured. Why don't you lose some weight? What do you do, eat all the time?"

Mack stood with her mouth open. She knew she was nothing to look at, but she had never had anyone, especially a child, talk to her like that. But, looking into the child's eyes, she could see the hurt and confusion behind the tough act.

"Looks like I'm gonna haf t' teach you some manners."

Mack moved toward Sam and Sam backed away. Billy ran to stand between the two. "Don't hit her, Mack," Billy said.

"Shame on ya, I mean you! I'd never hit anyone smaller than me. Especially someone scart as her."

Turning to Sam, she said, "Iffn ya want to travel with us, ya gots t' be respectful. Can ya do that?"

Sam hesitated as if weighing her options. Then she nodded her agreement.

Mack moved to her and hugged her to her ample belly. Then, turning to Billy she said, "Come on over here, boy."

Billy moved to embrace Mack. His small arms spread wide as he tried to put his arms around her.

"We's in this together, Gawd hep us," she said as she hugged the two youngsters to her belly. Then stepping back abruptly, as if embarrassed by her show of affection, she said, "Will, let me gits a few minutes sleep an then we'll talk about food." She looked at Sam as if challenging her to talk about her eating habits once more.

As Mack dozed off and started snoring, Sam whispered to Billy, "You know what? Mack is all right."

CHAPTER 23

The two couples were still in Key Largo. Besides lying on the beach, eating and sleeping, they had done nothing else. Their hearts were not in this trip. Billy was on everyone's mind. As they were gathered around the table lingering over coffee from breakfast, Wade's cell phone rang. Without comment, he got up and walked outside.

When he came back in, he was studying notes he had made in the small notepad he kept in his pocket. "Well, the sheriff in a place called Salt Cove, Florida, thought they had a break. One of the trucks they stopped at one of their road blocks contained a child's sneaker…"

Wade had to wait for the gasps and comments of distress before he continued. "The truck was an eighteen wheeler, one of those that carry cars. It was driven by a woman by the name of Machida Ruskin. She claimed that the shoe belonged to her little girl. They brought her into the sheriff's office and questioned her while they processed her truck. They found a small amount of blood in the heel of the sneaker, maybe from a blister that had popped. They

116

ran the blood type and it matched the blood type on Ms. Ruskin's driver's license. They let her go and there has been nothing else."

"Damn," said Robert. "It's as if the kid has disappeared into thin air." He heard sniffling and looked at his wife. "Are you okay, Sarah, honey? Remember the baby."

"Are you afraid I'm going to lose this one too, Robert? Are you going to blame me if I do? You going to blame me again?"

Robert got tears in his eyes. Sarah had lost a baby just before the Baptism Murders and Robert had blamed her. They had almost split up over it. He was now shocked that she would bring that up. He thought she had forgiven him.

Judith had been a big source of emotional support for the couple during the Baptism Murder Case when Sarah had been seeing the killer in her dreams. She now put her hands on their arms. "We're all on edge right now. We're all worried about Billy. I'm sure she didn't really mean that, did you, Sarah?"

"I'm sorry, Robert," Sarah said. "I love you and I have forgiven you."

He leaned over and kissed her.

"I'll tell you what," Wade said as he started clearing the table. "Why don't we go ahead and rent that lobster boat and see if we can catch us some lobster."

"They're not lobster, Wade," Judith teased. "They're giant crawfish."

"Well, y'all can call them whatever you want, but the one I had for supper last night tasted just like the one I had in Maine."

This got a big laugh from everyone. While they were laughing, Judith got on her I-pad to look for a boat.

CHAPTER 24

"Some honeymoon," Judith said as she tried to open her eyes and wake up at 4:00 a.m. the next morning. "It's still dark outside."

Wade laughed. "Here, honey. I brought you coffee with cream and sugar just like you like it."

"With Chickory?"

"Sorry, Babe. I couldn't find any of that kind of coffee here. Come on. Get dressed. We need to meet the boat in half an hour. I let you sleep as long as I could."

She stretched, yawned, and jumped out of bed. Grabbing a pair of cutoffs, tee shirt, and underwear that she had laid out the night before, Judith got dressed and headed for the bathroom. Wade sat on the bed and waited for her.

Coming out of the bathroom, brushing her hair, she said, "Wade, how do we catch the lobster? Do we use a net, or what?"

"I don't know. The crew on the boat will outfit us and show us what to do. Are you ready to go?"

She grabbed her sneakers and started for the door. "I'll put these on in the car."

"You'd better put them on now. We're going to be walking down to the dock. It's not that far, remember?"

Without a word, Judith sat down in the middle of the living room floor and put them on, without socks, and hurriedly laced them. Robert and Sarah were sitting on the porch, drinking coffee, and waiting for them. Walking down to the boating dock, they laughed and joked, but underneath it all they were thinking about Billy. After stopping by the Florida Fish and Wildlife, on the way, and getting a license, they jumped on board.

The captain welcomed them and introduced them to some of the crew. He then began the instructions for catching a Florida Spiny Lobster.

"Okay, here's what going to happen. After you're outfitted with diving equipment, you'll be given a tickle stick, a net, a pair of gloves and a gauge. What you need to know about the lobster is that it walks slowly forward. If it's scared, then it will flex its tail, causing a flipper-like motion, and jet backward at high speed. What you want to do is to find one hiding in a hole or under some coral.

"Take your tickle stick; slide it behind the lobster, gently tapping it on its tail. It will slowly walk forward. Place the net behind the lobster and tap it on the forehead. It will shoot backward into the net. Take it out of the net, make sure you have your gloves on, and measure it with this gauge. If it fits between the two arms, it's too small. You'll have to toss it back. Don't worry; some of the crew will be down there with you. Y'all have any questions?"

They looked at each other and shook their heads. The crew helped them with the wetsuits and accompanied them over the side.

The captain stared out over the water, lost in thought. A man came from below deck wearing a pair of overalls. He was thin with broad shoulders, wearing a long wig tied back in a pony tail, a cap pulled down low on his forehead, a fake beard, and sunglasses.

"Who are they?" the thin man asked.

Turning slowly, the captain looked at Kenneth Sunders, his brother. "They smell like cops to me, even one of the women. The one that's not pregnant."

"You think they're looking for me?"

"The man named Wade Russell said he and his wife are on their honeymoon. They invited the other couple to come to the Keys with them. But, you never can tell. You can't trust lawmen, can you?"

Kenneth eyed his brother, the brother he hadn't see in 35 years, the brother he thought was dead. He wondered what Rafe had been up to during the missing years. "Where did you go after you left home?" Kenneth asked. "How could you do that to our mother, just leave her like that?"

"Hold on there, little brother. You don't know the whole story. You were only six, how could you know what was happening?"

"I know we had it tough. I know you could have helped us. Did you know that there were nights when mama and I went to bed hungry? Mama said you promised dad, on his death bed, that you would take care of us."

Rafe lit a cigarette with shaky hands. Inhaling deeply and blowing the smoke out through his nose, he said, "I was sixteen years old. I stayed as long as I could, delivering papers before school and cutting lawns on weekends. Rachael, your mama, could have gotten a job and helped out. When she married dad, she thought she had married a rich man. She didn't realize, until after his death, that he had gambling debts. She expected me to drop out of school and work to pay off the debts and keep her in jewels and fine clothes. She hated me, Kenneth. I wasn't her kid, you know."

"What? I never knew that. So, we're half brothers. How did you survive on your own?"

Rafe grunted. Tossing the cigarette butt over the side of the boat, he turned to face Kenneth. "I lived on the street, stealing, eating out of garbage cans, going from one town to the next, until I met Squirrel. He saved my life but got me on the wrong side of the law. I was arrested and locked up in Juvey Hall so many times, I lost count.

"Just before I turned 18, I was lucky enough to go before Judge Renwick. He told me that if I messed up again, I would be put into adult prison. He was a judge who believed in trying to find solutions for troubled teens, instead of just punishing them. He had a brother, who owned a dude ranch in Wyoming. The judge sent kids out there to work if he thought he saw potential in them. I loved working the ranch. The work was hard and there were many rules, the biggest was not to mess with his daughter, Elise. She was a beauty and a flirt. I tried to stay away from her, but she drove me crazy. She was always around.

"One day, while I was brushing down one of the mares, she came into the barn and starting kissing me. I'm only human. Her father found us in the hay loft and fired me on the spot. I had made good wages, and the meals and rooms were furnished, so I had saved everything I made.

"I emptied out my bank account and came to the Keys and bought this boat. I always wanted to live on the water. In a way, I'm living daddy's dream. He always wanted to live on a boat."

Kenneth laughed. "It must be in our blood. It was the first place I thought of when I went on the run. It's amazing how we found each other."

Rafe nodded. "Yeah it was amazing. When I got out of my car, to change my flat tire, and you came barreling over that sand dune, I thought I was fixing to get robbed. I would have never known who you were with that disguise."

Kenneth fingered his fake beard and smiled. "It's a good thing we look so much alike. I knew who you were right away. I was shocked that you were still alive."

"Why did you think I was dead?"

"Mama told me. It's the way she explained your absence after you took off. I guess, to her, you were dead."

"Well, I don't have to worry about her anymore, but we do need to find your boy. Right now, you need to go below. The diving party will be back soon."

CHAPTER 25

Mack went to the office to get clean towels. She had waited until the manager had gone home for the day. The skinny, pimply faced boy was behind the desk. She thought he wouldn't question her. Billy told her about the maid coming by every morning to clean the room.

"I told her Mama was sick, but I don't think she believed me," he had said.

Mack had put a *do not disturb* sign on the door after that. Now she walked down to the office every evening to pick up towels. The kids were getting restless and tired of staying in the one room cabin, but Mack thought they should lay low for at least a couple more days.

Tonight, after everyone had their baths, she was going out to pick up pizza and Cokes. She had bought a DVD player earlier today and would rent a movie. It wasn't good for the kids to be inside all the time like this. They needed to be out playing. Of course Sam thought she was too old to play outside. She tried to talk Mack into buying her some makeup and high heels.

The towels were sitting on the counter waiting for her. The kid never looked up from his textbook. Mack carried the towels to the cabin and used her key to enter. She found Sam curled up on the bed they shared, face to the wall, crying her heart out. As Billy watched her, his bottom lip trembled.

"Now whut's all this? Whassa matter wit you two?" Mack asked, looking from one to the other.

"We were watching a movie and she started wailing," Billy said.

"Whut movie?"

"I don't know the name of it, but there was this girl who lived with her mama. There was no daddy. The mama kept giving herself shots and then she died. "

"It was heroin, you idiot," Sam screamed. Then she started crying again, her shoulders shaking.

Mack sat down on the bed. When she reached for her, Sam threw herself into her arms, crying loudly. Mack held her, pushing her hair out of her face. When Sam finally pulled away, Mack took the corner of her shirt and wiped her eyes.

"Is it the way ya mama died?"

Sam nodded. "I couldn't ma…ma…make her stop. No matter w…w…what I did."

"Well cours ya cuden," Mack said. "Ya jus a lil ole thang. It ain't yor fault."

Billy had been watching, wide eyed. "What's heroin?" he asked.

Mack laid Sam gently down on the bed and looked at Billy. "It's a bad drug." That's all the explanation she gave. "Bring me my purse over thor, Boy. I want to see iffn I needs ta go to tha cash machine affor I go git the pizza."

Billy picked up the heavy black bag and handed it to Mack. Once she counted her money, she pulled herself off the bed and headed for the door. Opening the door, she looked at Sam before closing it behind her. Sam had fallen asleep.

"Sho is a lot of damaged kids in tha worl," She said as she climbed into her truck.

Billy sat on his bed and watched Sam. She didn't seem so tough anymore. "A lot of kids have been hurt," he said. "We need to do something about it."

Sam looked at him with swollen eyes. Wiping her eyes with the heel of her hand, she said, "You're right, kid. Mack will help us."

Mack came back with a large pepperoni pizza, two large cokes and Jurassic Park to watch while they ate. The two youngsters had never seen the movie. They were so caught up in it that they almost forgot the pizza. Mack had to keep reminding them to eat. She ate very little herself. She seemed lost in thought. When the movie was over, she told them to brush their teeth and go to bed.

Pacing around outside the cabin with cell phone in hand, Mack called her mama. "Hey, Mama, it's me."

"Whor are ya, Mack? We bin worit to def bout ya. Ya still down in Florida? Ya needs ta git home. Annie is stil havin them nightmires."

"Look, Mama. I ran into some complications. I have two run-aways on my hands."

"Whut about ya own kid, Mack? She needs ya here."

"Annie's goin ta be okay, Mama. Now listen. Ya got any money left?"

"We got enough, don worry bout that."

"Ya got enough to get bus tickets to Florida?"

"I think so. When ya want us to leave?"

"Right now. Pack as much as ya kin and leave tha rist. It ain't worth much anyways. It'll take ya bout three days to get down ere. I'll meet ya in Key Largo."

"Why thor?"

Mack shrugged. "It's as good a place as any, Mama."

CHAPTER 26

Wade and Robert were sitting on the porch of the beach house they had rented, drinking coffee, and waiting for the women to wake up.

"I'm sure glad you and Sarah joined us on this trip, Robert," Wade said.

Robert took a large gulp of his coffee and set it on the table between them. "Sarah and I are having a good time. Catching all of those lobsters were the highlight of the trip. They were delicious, and I think we have enough in the freezer for another two meals. I love this place. As far as I'm concerned, we could stay here for the rest of the time. Did y'all especially want to drive all the way to Key West?"

"You know what, Robert? I was just thinking the same thing. It's so relaxing here. By the way, I checked in with the FBI, first thing this morning, and there is still no word about Billy." Wade stared out over the ocean and then looked at Robert. Robert looked deep in thought also. Looking at his watch, Wade said, "Are those girls going to sleep all day?"

"I'm up," Sarah said, coming out on the porch with coffee in hand. "Anyone need a refill?"

"Well, as long as you're up," Robert said, holding his cup out.

She put her cup down on the table. Then she held her hand out to Wade and he handed her his. "Thanks, Sarah," he said.

When the three were settled down on the porch, Sarah said, "I had one of those dreams last night."

They didn't need to ask what she meant. When Wade and Judith had gone to Monroe Beach to work on the Baptism Murders, Sarah was having dreams about the murderer. She also had visions of the girls being murdered. The stress was so great that one of her four personalities came out; the three year old little girl named Beth.

They now watched her as she gathered her thoughts. Sitting in the swing, she drew her legs up under her and took a deep breath.

"There was a tall thin man with a long ponytail and beard, wearing overalls, dark glasses, and a cap. He was with Billy, but I couldn't tell where they were. The background was fuzzy as if I was viewing them under water."

"I slept like a log," Judith said, coming out to join them and interrupting their train of thought. Leaning over and giving Wade a kiss, she then sat on his lap and took his coffee. Making a face she said. "Ugh, black coffee."

"Honey, Sarah was telling us about her dream," Wade said.

"Oh, I'm sorry. Go ahead, Sarah."

After she repeated her dream, Judith said, "Wait a minute. I saw a man like that on the boat, yesterday. Y'all didn't see him. I was the first one up the ladder and I caught a glimpse of him as he was going down below. I didn't think anything about it at the time. Was his hair salt and pepper colored, Sarah?"

"Yes it was."

"Wade, get that picture of Kenneth Sunders. I want to look at it, because now that I think about it, I think that's who that was on the boat. Sarah, once again, I think your dream just might help us solve this case."

"I'm worried," Sarah said. "Judith, do you think my personalities will split off again, now that I'm having these kinds of dreams again?"

"I don't think you have anything to worry about, Sarah. You're much stronger now than you were back then. You're not missing any time, are you?"

"No, I'm not."

Once Wade came back with the picture, Judith went to work with a magic marker, sketching in a beard. "I wish Julia was here," she said. "She's the artist."

"How is your twin, anyway?" Robert asked.

"She's doing great, her, the professor and all three kids."

"Here, look," She said, holding the picture up.

Sarah gasped. "That's him!"

CHAPTER 27

The captain of the boat had introduced himself as Captain Rafe. They had assumed it was his last name. They never thought to ask. His role was to take them out to catch lobster. Like many people they ran across in life, his name wasn't important. He served his purpose, was paid for the day and the two couples had gone on their way, never giving him a second thought.

After they had studied the picture of Kenneth Sunders, Wade and Robert headed back down to the dock to speak to the captain. The two girls went shopping. Sarah was hoping to find ideas for her upscale boutique on Monroe Beach.

"Uh oh," Rafe said when he saw the two men coming toward his boat. Looking around him, he made sure that Kenneth was below. Motioning for one of the crew to come near, he whispered, "Go below and make sure my brother stays put."

The man turned toward the ladder without a word. The crew had been working for Rafe for many years and obeyed without question.

"Ahoy, Captain!" Wade said. "Permission to come aboard."

"Permission granted," Rafe said with a big smile on his face. "You want to book another cruise?"

Wade decided to get right to it. Showing his badge, he said, "Wade Russell, FBI. Can we ask you some questions?"

"Sure," Rafe said. *That's never a good sign.*

Pulling out the picture of Kenneth Sunders, Wade said, "I believe you have this man working on your boat. He's probably wearing a wig and fake beard. We'd like to talk to him."

Wade was good at reading people. He studied the captain as Rafe looked at the picture.

Handing the picture back, he said, "He's not on my boat. All of my crew has been with me for years. I know them well."

"He would have probably signed on less than a month ago. Look at the photo again and make sure."

The captain shook his head. "As I said, my crew has been with me for years. I haven't hired anyone new."

Wade put the picture back in his pocket. "Do you mind if we look around?" he asked.

"Do you have a warrant?"

"No, but we can get one," Wade said.

Until then Robert had remained silent. Now he said, "If you have nothing to hide, then why do we need a warrant?"

"It's the principle of the thing," the captain said, jutting his chin out. "It's the principle of the thing."

Robert looked into his eyes and nodded. Then, without taking his eyes off Rafe, he said, "Wade, why don't I stay here while you go get a warrant?"

"Sure thing, Robert."

"You can't stay on my boat," The captain said. He was beginning to sound hostile.

"No problem, I'll wait on the dock," Robert said, holding both palms out.

After Wade left, Robert called Sarah while pacing up and down the dock. "Hi, honey. Y'all having a good time?"

"We sure are," said Sarah. "I'm getting a lot of good ideas for my boutique, and I found the most darling bikini for when I'm skinny again."

Robert laughed. "Okay, y'all shop til you drop. Wade went to get a warrant to search the boat, so I'm stuck here watching to make sure no one gets off. The captain's being difficult."

"Judith, you should get that. It looks so good on you. I'm sorry, Robert. Good luck. We need to continue our shopping."

"Okay, y'all have fun." As Robert disconnected, he heard the motor of the boat start up. He had been facing away from the boat, but now ran, with the intention of jumping on board. The boat took off at top speed.

"Damn it," Robert said as he angrily punching buttons on his cell phone. He was trying to call Wade but it went to voice mail. Looking up the number for the Coast Guard on his iPhone, he hurriedly ran his fingers over the keys.

CHAPTER 28

"You younguns git out ta bed. We leaving today." Mack grabbed the covers off both beds.

The kids hurriedly jumped up. "Oh, boy," Billy said. "Where we going, Mack?"

"We goin ta Key Largo," Mack said, tossing items into suitcases. "Y'all jest brush ya teeth and get dressed. I'm on chuck these suitcases in the truck. We'll stop fer breakfast on down tha road."

Billy was so excited that he bounced up and down in the seat. Finally Mack had enough.

"Can it, boy!" she shouted. "I gotta stop at this here filling station up ahead. Why don't you younguns git out and run for awhile to work off some uh that nervous energy. First pump some gas while I go in and pay, Billy."

Mack paid while Billy put gas in the truck, and then she headed for the restroom. Sam and Billy chased each other around the parking lot until Sam started moving from one foot to the other.

"Is Mack going to hog the ladies room forever? I gotta go. What the hell's keeping her so long?"

Suddenly, Billy had to go too. He headed for the men's room. When he came out, Sam almost knocked him down trying to get in. When she came out, Mack was still in the ladies room. Pounding on the door, Sam yelled, "Hey, Mack, you all right in there?"

There was no answer. Sam tried the door and, to her surprise, it was unlocked. Mack was lying on the floor, just inside the door. The two youngsters looked at each other and then moved toward Mack. Her skin had a bluish tinge.

"Is she dead?" Billy asked.

Sam began to cry as she nodded her head. Then she said, "I bet she died of a heart attack. She was way too fat."

Billy wanted to be strong for Sam but his bottom lip trembled and he finally broke down and cried. He was crying so loud that Sam put her hand over his mouth.

"Be quiet, Billy," she said.

"We got to tell the man inside to call the police, Sam."

"No, we can't let anyone know about this. If the police come, they'll take us. They'll probably put us in foster homes."

"We can't just leave her here."

"I'm sorry, but we have to. We've got to go to Key Largo and find Annie and Mack's mama."

"How are we going to get there?"

"In Mack's truck."

Billy's eyes became big as baseballs. "You know how to drive?" he asked.

"I've never driven, but it can't be that hard." Studying the corpse, Sam then said, "She never carried a purse. She had a wallet in her back pocket, like men use. We're going to have to roll her over and get it. We'll need money."

Billy backed away and tried to open the door, but Sam grabbed his arm. "I need you to help me roll her over. Look, I know it's an awful thing to do, but just make your mind blank."

He couldn't make his mind blank. He cried as they struggled to roll her over. When the deed was finally accomplished, Sam pulled the wallet out of Mack's hip pocket and stuck it inside her shirt. Without looking back, they left the bathroom and ran toward the truck. Getting into the driver's side, Sam could barely see over the steering wheel. She reached over the back, where Mack kept a stack of pillows, and put two under her.

Billy watched as she tried to reach the pedals. He knew what she was going to say before she said it.

"You're going to have to sit on the floor and push the gas pedal down for me, Billy."

It didn't take long before they realized it wasn't going to work. Sam had to tell him when to push the accelerator and when to hit the brakes. At one point, they were halfway into an intersection before Billy got the truck stopped.

"Okay, gently mash down on the gas pedal, while I aim toward the curb, Billy. I think we need to ditch the truck and find a bus."

He felt so relieved; he released his breath he hadn't known he was holding. "We need to use Mack's phone to get in touch with her mama, so we'll know where to go when we get to Key Largo."

"You're right, Billy," she said as she ran into the curb. "Get up off the damn floorboard and let's go."

When he got out of the truck, he looked around. "You going to leave it right here in the middle of the road?"

"Yep. I'll leave the keys in it and maybe someone will steal it."

"That's terrible," Billy said.

"Well, you can move it if you want, but I'm not driving it one more inch. Come on, get your stuff. We'll leave Mack's here."

They were in a subdivision with block houses on each side, painted in pastels colors. Huge oak trees lined both sides of the street.

"Get up here on the sidewalk. You look like an idiot walking out there," Sam said.

"Don't call me an idiot, you stupid bitch," he said as he jumped up on the sidewalk.

She took a deep breath. "I'm sorry, Billy." Looking around, she sighed. "Wonder which way the bus station is."

They kept walking and soon came to the center of town. The bus station was about a block down, on the other side of the street.

Sam pulled a twenty out of Mack's wallet and approached the ticket agent.

"Two children's tickets to Key Largo, please."

The man peered over the counter and asked, "Are you both under 12 years old?"

"Yes sir," Sam said.

He peeled off two tickets and took the twenty. Giving her back $2.13, he said, "The bus leaves in 20 minutes, from lane two."

They took seats near the back. Sam let Billy have the window seat. She felt guilty for snapping at him. Soon, a tiny little old lady sat down in the aisle seat across from them. Sam looked at her and she smiled. Sam quickly looked away.

"Where are you headed, dear?" the lady asked.

Sam pretended she didn't hear her. Billy leaned across Sam and said in a loud voice, "We're going to Key Largo!"

Sam poked him in the ribs and glared at him but he pretended he didn't notice.

"Are you two traveling alone?" the old lady asked.

Before Billy could answer, Sam said, "No, our parents are up front."

The old lady strained her neck, looking toward the front. Sam rolled her eyes as she looked at Billy. "Pretend to sleep," she whispered.

Billy closed his eyes but his eyelids fluttered so much, he knew the old lady would know he was pretending. Sam closed her eyes and made soft snoring noises, but the lady wasn't fooled by either of them.

"My name is Miss Baker," she said.

Sam opened her eyes and glared at her but Billy felt sorry for her and didn't want to hurt her feelings.

"My name's Billy and this is Sam. We're on vacation."

"In October?"

"Uh, yeah, well it's winter break."

"Oh, that's nice. When I was a child we didn't have winter and spring breaks. We only got out of school in the summer."

"Who cares," Sam said under her breath.

Billy looked quickly at Miss Baker to see if she had heard Sam, but she didn't seem to hear. Miss Baker was thinking that these two were by themselves, that they had no parents up front. They were probably runaways. She decided to watch them when they got off the bus and see if they were alone. She had plans for them.

CHAPTER 29

Robert was arguing with the Coast Guard authorities when Wade drove up. Robert hung up, cutting the dispatcher off in mid sentence.

Getting out of the car, Wade looked toward the dock. "Where did the boat go?"

"They took off. I've been trying to call you. According to the dispatcher at the Coast Guard, the FBI has no jurisdiction over them. They won't go after the boat just because we say there is a wanted man aboard."

"What, we going to have to get in a pissing contest with some dispatcher? I can't believe this."

Wade called the Coast Guard back. "Yeah, this is Wade Russell, with the FBI. I have a warrant for Kenneth Sunders, who we believe is on the boat with call numbers WACO 346-G. We need some help, here. Thanks."

Turning to Robert, he said, "They're sending out some boats now."

Robert didn't ask for any explanation. Getting the Coast guard out there was what was important. They heard a motor and looked up to see the boat in question headed toward the dock. The captain waved to them as if they were friends. After one of the crew tied the line, the captain told them to come aboard.

"It was the principle of the thing, before. I had given my word that the fellow you were looking for wasn't on board. I can be a hothead sometimes. You gentlemen are welcome to look around. You don't need a warrant."

Wade looked at Robert and nodded. "He's dropped him off somewhere. It's not going to do any good to search the boat, but let's do it anyway. It's the principle of the thing, after all," he said winking. "First let me call off the Coast Guard."

Calling the Coast Guard, Wade told them what had happened. He told them how long the ship had been gone. They agreed to scan the area around the coast and in some of the tiny islands off Key Largo, based on the time frame. After going over the boat and thanking the captain, the two men headed off to meet Sarah and Judith.

They found them walking toward the cottage, their arms loaded with shopping bags. They were laughing and talking and didn't notice that Wade had pulled the car over to the curb in front of them.

"You two sexy women want a ride with two hunks?" Wade asked, getting out and taking the packages from them.

"Did you catch him?" Judith asked, as she got into the back seat beside Sarah.

"Nope," said Wade. "The damn captain took off, dropped him off somewhere, and came back, giving us permission to search his boat."

"Wonder why he would protect him?" Judith said. "Are they longtime friends, or maybe brothers?"

"I don't know," Robert said. "The Coast Guard are on alert, so we have help. The captain could have dropped him off on one of the other islands. Billy is still missing also. It's like looking for a needle in a haystack."

CHAPTER 30

Kenneth was on the run again. It was bad luck that the lobster party, a couple of days ago, had been two FBI agents and the sheriff of some bumfuck town in Georgia. Rafe had dropped him on the other side of the island. He had ditched the wig and beard, picked up some red dye and reading glasses at the local general store, and found a cheap motel, paying cash for the room. He was now a red headed guy with a buzz cut and reading glasses. He practiced several ways of walking in front of the mirror and decided to walk with a stoop. He then took some talcum powder from his suitcase and powdered it over his eyebrows, eyelashes and hair.

Lying on the broken down bed, he thought about Billy. Now that he knew Billy was no longer with the sheriff of Monroe Beach, he was worried. He could be anywhere.

"Maybe I should turn myself in. It doesn't matter anyway, now that I can't see Billy," he mumbled to himself.

Picking up the remote from the nightstand, he turned on the TV and started flipping through channels. He saw several football games, some game shows, Judge Judy, and old movie with Doris Day and Rock Hudson, and finally a news channel. He watched news about Iran, and the rest of the Middle East, another school shooting out in Oklahoma, and then the local fishing, news, and weather. He saw nothing about himself.

Just as he was starting to turn off the TV, an announcer came on with a special news bulletin. The announcer was a perky young blonde, smiling, showing all of her teeth. She was standing in front of a filling station. Trying to sound serious, she quit smiling and said, "The lady who was found earlier on the floor of the ladies room behind me has been identified as Mack Ruskin, a truck driver from Enid, Texas. According to the owner, she came in with a girl around 13 and a boy around eight. They apparently drove off in the pickup truck they had arrived in, leaving Ms. Ruskin lying on the floor of the ladies room. Ms. Ruskin died of a heart attack, but the police are looking for the two youngsters. The boy is believed to be Billy Sunders who had been on an Amber

Alert for several days. This is the picture we have of Billy Sunder, but we don't yet know the identity of the girl. If you see this boy, who may be with an older girl, call the number on your screen."

Kenneth felt better, but not much. If they were together, then they had a better chance of surviving, but they were still just kids out there alone. He picked up the phone book on the nightstand and looked up the FBI.

As soon as someone answered the phone, he said, "My name is Kenneth Sunders. I'm wanted by the FBI. I want to turn myself in."

CHAPTER 31

Miss Baker's short fat legs moved down the aisle of the bus, slowly. She couldn't move as fast as the youngsters. Craning her neck, she tried to see over the heads in front of her. Billy and Sam had squeezed through the crowd and stood near the front.

Putting on her helpless little old lady act, she said in a feeble voice, "Please let me through. My grandkids are up front and I need to catch up with them."

The tall man in front moved aside and made way for her, telling the others to do the same. She was soon behind the children. They didn't notice her and bounded off the bus, not bothering with the steps. She watched as they stood in the parking lot looking around as if they didn't know what to do or where to go.

Both Billy and Sam jumped when they heard a voice behind them say, "May I help you kids? Your parents seem to have disappeared. They weren't on the bus, were they?" They stared, open mouthed and she continued, "You don't have to be afraid. I can see you're alone. I just want to help."

"We don't need any help," Sam said. "We just need to call our grandmother and little sister and let them know we're here."

"Oh, okay, dear. May I offer you a ride or is your grandmother picking you up?"

Without a word, Sam walked away, looking at the contacts on Mack's cell phone. There were so few she was able to identify the mama right away. There was no answer. Disconnecting, she looked around and saw Billy still talking to Miss Baker.

"She's on her way," Sam said as she walked back over to where they were.

"I'll just wait with y'all until she gets here, then."

The bus station in Key Largo was small. Before long, there were no buses or people around. There was one man inside, reading a cheap paperback. He never looked up as a long black Lincoln Town Car pulled in front with darkened windows. A tall, broad shouldered man with metal teeth got out and opened the back door.

"Oh, here is my ride," Miss Baker said as she moved toward the car.

Billy was sad to see the lady go, but Sam was relieved. The youngsters watched as she waved goodbye. It puzzled them that the chauffeur didn't close the back door. He glanced inside and looked around. Then he moved so fast that they didn't have time to act. He grabbed both kids and, in one swift motion, threw them into the back seat, slamming the door. Billy looked for handles, none. They were trapped.

Sam started screaming as the limo pulled into the street. Miss Baker slapped her across the mouth, splitting her top lip. Blood poured down her chin.

"I know you think I'm just a stupid old lady, but I will demand respect from you two. I saw you on TV last night," she said, looking at Billy. "You're a long ways from Nashville. And you, miss big mouth, haven't been reported as missing, as far as I can tell. Jupiter would be proud of me, if she were still alive."

"Who's Jupiter?" Billy asked.

The old lady laughed. "Your friend, Judith McCain could tell you who Jupiter was. Jupiter killed her husband. I was one of her lieutenants. We had a good thing going until Dr. McCain, Wade Russell, and Tracy Carr messed everything up. They thought

Jupiter had turned us all over, in exchange for being sentenced to a mental hospital for the criminally insane. But she didn't turn her major officers over to the FBI. She kept some of us in reserve, as bargaining chips in case she ever got caught again. She contacted me when she escaped, but before we could get our operation going again, Wade Russell killed her."

"What kind of operation?" Sam asked.

Miss Baker looked at her long and hard, but didn't answer. Sam was getting more and more scared. She thought she was beginning to understand what they had in mind. She looked at Billy. He looked so sweet and innocent that it broke her heart. She decided that she would have to protect him at all cost.

Driving down a white sandy road with scrub brush on each side, they finally came to a big house. When Miss Baker saw them studying it, she explained, "That's coquina. It's ground up shells and is used to build houses in Florida and the Keys."

When the chauffeur opened the rear door, Sam ducked under his arm and ran, but he was too fast for her. He grabbed her by her hair and dragged her, kicking and screaming, inside the house. At the same time, Miss Baker pulled Billy against her, wrapping her arms around him. She held him until the driver came back out.

"Okay, Buzz, get this one inside and then tell Winnie to come help me with their things."

Buzz pulled Billy by both arms and fast-stepped him inside. He caught a glimpse of a huge foyer, a formal dining room off to the side, and a chandelier as he was shoved up the stairs. Taking a key from his pocket, Buzz unlocked a door and pushed him inside. It was an oversized room with bunk beds along three walls. Sam was sitting on a lower bunk with her arm around a small, red haired, freckled faced girl who was crying.

"This is Annie," Sam said. "She said that they took her and her granny when they got off the bus. This is Billy, Annie."

Annie ground her fist into her eyes before raising her head and looking at Billy. His tender heart melted when he looked into her green eyes. "Did you see my granny when they brought you in?" she asked.

"No, I didn't. What are we going to do, Sam?"

Sam stood and began to pace the room. Walking to the window, she tried to open it, but it was nailed shut. "If we can find something to get these big nails out of the window, we could jump down."

Billy and Annie went to the window and looked out. All they saw was a pile of white sand with a few scrub bushes growing in it.

"Well," said Billy, "I guess those weird looking bushes would break our fall, but we're going to get scratched mighty bad. None of them have leaves."

Sam looked at him like he had lost his mind. "You rather get scratched a little or be sold as a child prostitute?"

Annie's eyes widened. "What's a prostut?"

Sam studied them both. They were so young and innocent. She would do anything to protect them. "Never mind," she said. "You don't need to know. We'll be long gone before they can sell us."

"But, what about granny?" Annie said, her bottom lip trembling.

"We'll have to leave her for now," Sam said.

Billy gasped, "What are you talking about, Sam? We can't leave her here."

Sam put her hands on his shoulders. "Billy, they won't do anything to her. She's too old. They can't get any money for her. Once we get out, we'll come back for her," she lied. "Now, help me find something to knock these nails out."

CHAPTER 32

Kenneth Sunders was taken back to Nashville to stand trial for the murder of Rose Sunders. He couldn't afford a lawyer and was assigned a public defender, Linda Foley. She was a tall slim woman with thick black frizzy hair. When they brought Kenneth from his cell, she stood to shake his hand. She noticed that he was wearing a red jumpsuit and knew he was on suicide watch.

He didn't make eye contact as she extended her hand. "I'm Linda Foley, your attorney."

"I don't need an attorney," he said. "I murdered my wife and now I want to be put to death. I don't deserve to live."

He sat down with a heavy sigh while she opened a folder and started reading. This was her first case, she had only passed the bar exam a month before. She wanted to win and make a name for herself. She didn't want to be a public defender forever. Mr. Sunders had given the police very little information, but, from what she could tell, she thought she could make a good case of not guilty by reason of temporary insanity.

She cleared her throat. "Mr. Sunders, you are being charged with manslaughter. When we go in for the arraignment, I want you to plead not guilty by reason of insanity."

He looked up and into her eyes. He had never seen eyes that color before. They were bright emerald green. She was beautiful. He studied her for a moment, and then shook his head. "Nope. I killed Rose in cold blood. I knew what I was doing. I wasn't insane."

"Mr. Sunders…"

"Call me Kenneth."

"Kenneth, you can call me Linda. Look, Kenneth, your kid was missing, you were under a lot of stress, and then you found out that your wife knew he was missing hours before you did. I suspect that your wife was abusing him also, which was probably why he ran away. Billy is going to need you, when they find him."

"No, they're not going to find him. It's hopeless."

She took both of his hands. "Look at me, Kenneth."

When he looked up, he saw tears in her eyes. She really did care. Maybe there was hope. He slowly nodded, "You're right. I've been thinking only of myself. I need to beat this and find Billy. What do you want me to do?"

She smiled and become even more beautiful to him.

CHAPTER 33

"Y'all see any sense in staying around here?" Wade asked as he accepted another cup of coffee from Judith. "Now we know that Kenneth Sunders has turned himself in and no telling where Billy is. What do y'all want to do?"

"We need to be heading back to Monroe Beach soon," Robert said. "But y'all go ahead and stay if you want. You don't need us for the rest of your honeymoon."

Wade laughed, "Are you forgetting we rode down together, Sheriff?"

"No, I'm not forgetting. Sarah and I talked about this last night. We want to drive up the coast, all the way to Monroe Beach, maybe stop off in St. Augustine for a few days. Y'all can rent a car out of Miami. I already called and they will deliver one to you this afternoon."

Wade shook his hand. "Okay. It's been fun having y'all here with us. Judith and I will probably hang around for a few more days and then head on back to Houston. I don't see any sense in going all the way to Key West. We love it here."

After they helped Sarah and Robert pack their car, Wade and Judith walked back inside the cabin with their arms around each other. When they got inside, Wade pulled her to him, giving her a long deep kiss.

"Now that we're alone, how about a little afternoon delight?" he asked.

"Hey, it works for me," she said as she ran toward the bedroom.

CHAPTER 34

They had been served bowls of clam chowder in their room by Annie's granny. After unlocking the door, Buzz watched them like a hawk. He had brought in a table and four chairs. Annie had run over and hugged her grandmother after the food was laid out on the table. Billy and Sam had watched with tears in their eyes.

After the grandma and Buzz left, the kids dug in. When Sam turned up her glass of sweet iced tea to drink, Billy reached over and grabbed a piece of paper that was stuck to the bottom. He read the note out loud.

Annie, If you can get out, don't worry about me. I can't stand to think of what will happen to you if you stay here. Love you, Granny.

Billy looked at the window and then down at his tea glass. It was heavy crystal. "Hey, y'all," he said. "We got to figure out a way to keep one of these glasses. We don't need to take the nails out of the window. We can break it."

Sam looked at the glass and weighed it in her hand. "Yeah," she said, squinting at the window. "We have to wait until they leave.

If Annie's granny picks up our dishes, she won't tell anyone that we kept a glass or two. Let's stack the dishes together so Buzz won't notice."

They put one of the glasses in the closet. Once they stacked the glasses together, it was hard to tell how many were there. Soon Buzz escorted Granny in and watched while she gathered the dishes onto a tray. They left and the kids waited. They were later served supper, hamburger patties and yellow rice. Again, they hid one of the glasses, stacking the others. There was no TV, no games, puzzles, nothing to help pass the time. They spent most of their time looking out the window until they got tired and sleepy, then dozed on the bunk beds.

A bright light woke Billy up. He leaped off the bed in time to see the limo back out of the garage. Buzz got out and opened the rear door for Miss Baker.

"Hey, Sam," Billy said in a loud whisper. She jumped up and then Annie said, "What's wrong?"

"Shh," the other two said together and motioned for her to join them at the window. Sam and Annie got the glasses out of the closet. Annie handed hers to Billy. "On the count of three," he whispered.

The noise was so much louder than they had expected. They took towels to put around their hands to break the rest of the window pane out. Annie heard a key turning in the lock and ran over, standing in front of the door. A woman walked in.

"What in the hell do you kids think you're doing?" she asked. They stared, wide eyed. She was tall and so thin that she looked like a skeleton with skin stretched over it. What little hair she had was an unlikely yellow. Her eyes were squinting so tight it was hard to see what color they were.

Sam put her mouth next to Billy's ear. "I think we can take her," she whispered. Before they could act on it, Annie fell to her knees and bit the woman on her calf. She kicked back and her foot made contact with Annie's head. Annie fell on the floor and lay very still. Billy and Sam moved in and started punching the woman in the belly. She swatted at them as if they were mosquitoes. Both kids kicked her shins and punched her belly. She became enraged, screaming to the top of her lungs. Annie's granny ran in and picked Annie up, laying her on one of the beds. Annie opened her eyes and Granny put her fingers to her lips to be quiet.

Noticing a glass laying on the floor near the window, Granny picked it up, circled around in back of the thin woman, and hit her over the head. The children had to jump out of her way as she fell face down.

"Let's get out of here before Winnie wakes up," Granny said. "We've got to get the police in here. I heard them talking about picking up another shipment tonight. No telling how many kids they have had here and done no telling what with."

The kids had kept their clothes on in anticipation of leaving, but Granny was in her nightgown and slippers. Without bothering with shoes or a robe, she ushered the kids downstairs and into the kitchen. Pulling open a drawer near the sink, she searched until she found a set of keys.

"I kept my eyes open for any opportunity," she said as she held up the keys, grinning.

She led the children out a door, off the kitchen, into a garage. A beach buggy was the only vehicle in there. Granny hit a switch and the garage door opened. Billy and Sam got in the back, Granny in the driver's seat, and Annie rode shotgun. As she was backing out, Winnie flung the kitchen door open and ran toward the car. She had her hand on the passenger door when Granny put the pedal to the metal. The buggy shot back, throwing Winnie to the cement floor. Granny headed toward the beach. After a short distance, she drove over a large sand dune and the kids whooped with laughter. Granny joined in.

Parking on the beach, Granny cut off the engine, in front of a group of cottages. Turning in her seat, she looked at the kids.

"Y'all can call me Granny. Whut's your names?"

"I'm Sam and this is Billy."

"Let's get out of this crazy car," Granny said. "I think better when I'm pacing."

Annie followed her granny, but Billy motioned for Sam to follow him. Walking away from the others, Billy said, "They don't know about Mack."

Sam glanced at the other two. Both were walking with their heads down and their hands clasped behind their backs.

"Maybe we won't have to tell them," Sam said.

Billy frowned at her. "Of course we have to tell them."

Sam shook her head. "Nope, I'm not telling them. You can if you want to."

"Whut er you kids arguing about?" Granny said as she walked up behind them.

"Nothing," they said at the same time.

She looked from one to the other, and then shrugged. "Either of you have a cell phone?"

Without thinking, Sam said, "We had Mack's, but Buzz took it away from us." As soon as she said that, she put her hand over her mouth.

Annie and Granny stared at Sam as their jaws dropped. Then Granny said, "Whut happened ta Mack? Whut did ya do ta her?"

Billy had to stick up for Sam. In a loud voice he said, "We didn't do anything to her. She died of a heart attack." He started crying and Annie joined in. Soon, they were all standing on the beach crying.

Judith happened to be walking by the front window and glanced out, seeing Billy standing there with three other people.

"Wade, come here, look," She said pointing. "Isn't that Billy out there?"

He didn't bother to answer. Running through the living room and onto the porch, he jumped and hit the ground running. Judith was right behind him. The group on the beach noticed the couple just before they reached them. Recognition lit up Billy's face. He was so glad to see them that he forgot about the reason he had run away. Throwing himself into Judith's arms, he hugged her as tight as his little arms could hug. Everyone started talking at once.

There was so much confusion that Wade finally said, "Let's go inside. We're staying in that cabin over there."

"Will ya hep me hide this buggy?" Granny asked. "There's some bad people after us and this belongs ta them."

"Judith, take the kids inside and I'll help...what's your name?"

"Edith Ruskin, but call me Granny, everyone else does."

"Granny, I'm Wade Russell and this is Judith McCain. We both work for the FBI and we've been looking for Billy. It's amazing how things turn out sometimes."

"It's amazing," Granny said. "You're just the person we need right now. There's some bad stuff going on you need to know about."

"Come on, kids," Judith said and led them toward the cabin.

Wade and Granny pushed the beach buggy between the sand dunes and covered it with seaweed that had washed up on the beach during the night. When they got to the cabin, Judith and the kids were having cookies and milk.

"Y'all want sweet iced tea?" she asked.

When they nodded, she got up and started toward the kitchen. "Let's have it on the porch," Wade said. "Come on kids. Bring your milk out here." He picked up the plate of cookies and they followed.

When they were done eating, Wade said, "Okay, Billy, you start. Begin with when you ran away from us and don't leave anything out. Why did you run anyway?"

"Y'all were going to put me in a foster home."

When no one said anything, he continued, he told them the whole story. When he got to the part about Mack dying, the kids and Granny started crying.

Annie crawled into her granny's lap and hid her face on her shoulder. Granny patted her back. "I thought I should take her to one of them psychologist, but Mack said no, that the psychologist would call the police."

"I'm a psychologist," Judith said. "The only time we have to break confidentiality is when there is danger of the client hurting themselves or others. But we can talk later. Let's let Billy finish his story."

Billy continued his story. When he got to the part about Miss Baker, He said. "I thought she was a nice lady."

Sam interrupted. "Yeah she acted like a nice old grandma. But I wasn't fooled. Billy kept answering her questions, but I tried to ignore her. When we got down here, I tried to call Granny on Mack's cell phone, but no one answered. I told Miss Baker that our grandmother and little sister were picking us up, but I could tell she didn't believe me.

When her car got there, her chauffeur grabbed us and threw us in the back seat. They drove us to a big house and locked us in a room with lots of beds. Annie was in there."

"Granny, how did you and Annie end up there?" Judith asked.

"Well, we got on the bus back in Texas, where we're from, but had to change in Tallahassee. Miss Baker got on in Homestead. She sat across the aisle from us and started talking, asking us questions about where we were from, where we were going, you know like people do on trips. She kept looking at Annie and talking about how adorable she was. When the bus pulled into Key Largo, I asked her where we should go to find a room. She said her driver would drop us off at a motel on the way to her house. When we got in her limo she grabbed my purse, took my cell phone out, and smashed it. Her whole personality changed. We were trapped inside the car and she took us to the big house where she locked Annie in one of the rooms. She told me that I would do the cooking and if I tried to run, she would hurt Annie."

"She was a mean lady, all right," Billy said. "She said that she was a lieutenant of Jupiter and that…"

Judith gasped. "What did you say, Billy? Did you say Jupiter?"

"Yeah," Billy said. "She said she was continuing Jupiter's work. Oh, yeah, she said you would know who Jupiter was because Jupiter killed…"

"Yeah, she killed Ben," Judith said. "He was my husband. She also tried to kill me and almost succeeded."

No one said anything for awhile. The room was quiet as they watched Judith. She stared off into space and then she turned to Wade. "Honey, if she's continuing Jupiter's work that means she has a pedophile ring going on. I can't believe it's reached down this far. My God, Wade, just think, even after arresting all those judges and people in high places, we may have just scratched the surface."

"Yeah, we figured she held some names back, but she must have held back many more than we thought. Y'all excuse me. I need to make some calls."

CHAPTER 35

The judge didn't grant Kenneth Sunders bail, so he was held over for trial. That night he was allowed to receive a phone call. Wondering who the call could be from, he picked up the receiver in the hall. The voice on the other end said, "Dad?"

Kenneth's eyes watered when he recognized his son's voice. "Billy? Son, are you all right?"

Billy was laughing and crying at the same time. "I'm all right, Dad. I'm with Judith and Wade. They work for the FBI. I found them in Key Largo. I ran away from them and hid in a big truck, but Mack died and then Miss Baker took us prisoner. Granny busted us out and Judith and Wade found us. Miss Baker worked for Jupiter and now they're going to arrest her."

"Whoa, son, you're going too fast for me, but it's okay. I'm glad you're okay. Listen, I have a good lawyer and she thinks she can help me get a light sentence. I might not even have to serve time. Can you stay with Wade and Judith until I'm out, and then I can come get you?"

"You won't have to come get me, Dad. As soon as they wrap up this case down here, they're going to bring me there. They said to tell you not to worry about a thing. They said that I'll probably need me to testify about Rose hitting me. I love you, Dad."

"I love you too, Son. I've got to go."

Billy handed the phone back to Wade.

"I want you kids to stay here with Judith," Wade said. "Stay inside and don't let anyone in."

He put on a black jacket that said FBI on the back, grabbed his cell phone and keys, kissed Judith and headed out. Judith watched the SUV back out of the driveway.

When she turned away from the window, she saw Granny and the kids sitting on the couch watching her. "Who wants to help me bake cookies?"

They headed toward the kitchen and Granny asked, "Kin I hep, too?"

Judith put her arm around the small lady. "Actually, Granny, I was hoping you'd teach me. I don't have a mix and I know nothing about making anything from scratch."

Granny laughed. "Be glad ta teach ya. You bad as Mack." As she said that, tears rolled down her cheeks.

CHAPTER 36

Wade was pumped. He was to meet the other agents, including Simon, of the Atlanta office; and Tracy Carr, of the Houston office; at a convenience store a couple of blocks down from the big house where the kids had been held. He always felt an emotional high when he was on the verge of catching the bad guys. He hadn't been part of the team who had first captured Jupiter. It had taken the FBI close to two years to wrap the case up. When she had escaped, he had been the one to kill her. He couldn't believe that the evil she had started was still going on. He hated people who hurt children. Judith would want to be part of the interrogation. She would want to study Miss Baker and try to figure out what made her turn out the way she did. Wade didn't care why she did what she did. All he cared about was seeing that she was locked away for the rest of her miserable life.

Wade pulled around the back of the convenience store where the rest of the agents were. When Tracy saw him, she walked over and hugged him. "Glad we could be in on this one, Wade. How's my niece? Hell of a way to spend a honeymoon, huh?"

"Didn't expect to see you, Tracy, but I should have known you'd be here, after being so involved in the Jupiter case. Judith's fine. I left her back at the cabin, with some of the would-be victims of this old lady who calls herself Jupiter's lieutenant."

Tracy shook her head. "Seems like an endless battle. We're going to have to scare the crap out of the old lady, threaten her with the death penalty. We need to get them all this time, Wade."

He nodded, "I agree."

"Y'all ready to go?' Simon yelled.

Checking his revolver, Wade gave the a-okay sign.

The agents moved through the scrub brush in back of the store and circled around the back of the big house. They stayed low. Spreading out, they covered all sides of the building. As they watched, the limo pulled in. A tall man got out and opened the back door. Four children, ranging in ages of about three to 12 got out and looked around. The old lady followed, yelling for Winnie.

"Where is that girl?" they heard her say. "Buzz, get these kids inside and get them fed. Tell Granny to fix the clam chowder again. And watch out for Sam and Billy. They're tricky. They may have something planned. Well, what are you standing there for? Move!"

The group of agents knew to wait until the kids were separated from the criminals before they moved in. They also knew that, when they discovered the kids missing, they would be on the alert. The timing was going to be tricky. They didn't want to create a hostage situation.

Wade had questioned the kids and granny about the layout of the house and knew where they would put the new kids. He crawled on his belly and went in through the kitchen. He was relieved to know that there was no one in there. There was a staircase off the kitchen. Bounding up the stairs quietly, he reached the top. Ducking into an empty room, he left the door ajar and watched the hallway. Soon the new group of kids came up the main staircase, followed by the tall man. He watched the kids pass by. The tall man followed. Wade jumped him from behind, giving him a karate chop to the back of the neck. The man's knees buckled and he went down, not making much noise.

Wade dragged the man into the empty room where he had been hiding, took duck tape from his cargo pants and secured him. The kids were standing in the hallway. They looked lost.

Wade put his finger to his mouth, as a sign to be quiet and whispered, "Don't be afraid. I'm with the FBI. I want y'all to wait in here." He opened the door to the room where Billy, Sam, and Annie had been kept.

Getting on his walkie-talkie, he said, "The upstairs is secure, the kids are safe. As far as I can tell, the only person left downstairs is the old lady, but move in slowly.

As the agents moved toward the house, the limo pulled out and took off so fast that Tracy saw only a streak of black. She fired off several shots, but they made no impact on the car. The agents ran into the house and found no one. They found Winnie unconscious in the garage. Tracy called an ambulance. Checking for a pulse, she found a very weak one. She stayed with the woman and waited for the ambulance while the agents continued to search the rest of the house. When the ambulance arrived, the head agent out of Miami assigned one of his men to go to the hospital with the suspect, to guard her until she regained consciousness and could answer questions.

The island was small. Roadblocks were set up on the bridge leading to the mainland. Miss Baker wouldn't get far. No one was worried.

The new kids spoke Spanish and couldn't speak English. Tracy was fluent in Spanish. After questioning the kids, she found out that they had been picked up in El Paso, Texas, at the border to Mexico. They were orphans. They were promised that they would be adopted by American parents. Immigrations would have to sort out that problem. Wade headed back toward the cabin. He was now ready to get off this island and hoped Judith was ready too.

CHAPTER 37

Judith and Granny had made cookies and all that was left were crumbs. The kids were now restless and wanted to swim.

"Well, what do you think, Granny?" Judith said. "Wade said to stay inside, but I don't see any harm in going down to the beach. We'll keep a close watch on them. They probably already have everyone in custody by now anyway."

"I think it'll be all right. We kin jest go right thar across from the cabin. It looks like a right nice beach," Granny said.

"Okay, put on your swim suits."

"They ain't got none," Granny said. "We left everything in the big house. They'll haf ta swim in their underwear."

Sam refused to swim in her underwear. Judith gave her one of her new bikinis she had bought on her shopping spree with Sarah. It was big on Sam. Judith pinned it up with large safety pins. Sam loved the look. Walking down the small path toward the beach, they talked in excited voices. Judith thought she heard a car drive up in front of the cabin. Thinking it was Wade's car, she said, "My husband's not going to be happy about us coming out here."

Judith stopped , turned around and walked back, expecting to see Wade. Miss Baker was standing on the path with a gun in her hand. "I thought I recognized my three little ones coming out of the cabin back there. Just keep walking. I only need one of the children to help me get off this island. I'll take the little red headed girl."

The others had run ahead and didn't notice that Judith was in trouble. Granny moved fast for an old woman, having no problem keeping up with the children. Judith looked around, trying to find something to use to hit this lady with.

"Stop right here," Miss Baker said. "Sit down here behind the scrub bush so no one will see you."

Keeping the gun trained on Judith, Miss Baker lowered herself down next to her. "Okay, here's what I want you to do. You go get the little red headed girl and bring her back here. I'll keep the gun on you until you get back. I won't harm any of you unless you disobey me. If you disobey me I'll kill you all right here."

"How am I supposed to get Annie to come back here? She's wanted to swim all day. She's not going to come with me."

"Tell her you have some boogie boards up at the house that you need her to help you carry."

"I will not turn any of the kids over to you, Miss Baker."

"Then you will all die, except Annie. Once I kill the rest of you, I can take her anyway. Now go on down there and bring her back. Remember, I will have the gun pointed at your back."

Judith stood and started down the path.

When Wade got to the cabin, he was surprised to find no one there. He went to use the bathroom and then grabbed bottled water out of the fridge drinking it down. "They're probably down on the beach," he said to himself.

Walking onto the front porch, he scanned the area in the front of the cabin. Noticing the path leading down to the beach, he started across the yard and down the path. He heard voices. One sounded like Judith. He started to call out to her, but hesitated. He was glad he did. He saw her stand up and head down toward the beach. Then she looked back and he saw the barrel of a weapon point toward her. He didn't have to see the other person to know who it was. Pulling his own gun from his shoulder holster, he walked to his right and circled around so that he was behind the armed person.

He saw Miss Baker sitting on a small rise. She had her weapon trained on the path. She was actually smiling. He dove and knocked her over, knocking the breath out of her. Reaching for her gun, he wasn't fast enough and he felt a searing hot pain under his arm. Judith ran up in time to see Wade fall over, blood spilling on the white sand. It was like watching a replay of when Jupiter killed Ben. She froze for only a split second as Miss Baker re-aimed her forearm at Wade. Judith ran and kicked Miss Baker in the hand that was holding the revolver. Before Miss Baker could recover, Judith kicked her in the head. Tracy had trained her well. Without pausing, she kicked the gun into the bushes.

Miss Baker didn't move. Judith dropped to her knees to tend to Wade. "I'm okay. Cuff her, Judith," he said.

She had never secured anyone before. Fumbling around trying to get the cuffs off Wade's belt, they heard Miss Baker moan. Out of the corner of her eye, Judith saw her feeling around for the gun. Judith jumped up and kicked her in the head again. Wade laughed. He couldn't help it. Judith was a psychologist. She had never had to deal with this situation before.

Granny and the kids had heard the commotion and came running up from the beach in time to see Judith kick Miss Baker in the head. Judith finally got the cuffs off Wade's belt and turned Miss Baker face down while she cuffed her.

Wade pulled himself across the sand and turned Miss Baker's head so that she could breathe. He then got on his cell phone and called an ambulance and the other agents.

The bullet had grazed the skin around Wade's armpit. It was painful but not serious. The doctor offered him pain medication but he refused. He needed to keep a clear head to question Miss Baker.

The agents took Miss Baker to the sheriff's office. It was the only local law enforcement agency in Key Largo. They were greeted by Sheriff John Pepper, a tall muscular man in his forties. The interrogation room was small. The other agents went home except for Judith, Wade and Cole Jakes, head of the Miami FBI.

Everyone gathered around the small table, with Miss Baker seated in the middle of one side.

"Wade, why don't you lead the questioning, since you know more about Jupiter than any of us," Cole Jakes said. Everyone nodded.

Wade informed Miss Baker that the questioning would be recorded. She only nodded, still with a smirk on her face. He turned on the tape recorder and announced the date, time, and stated the full name of everyone present.

Before Wade could ask the first question, Miss Baker said, "You'll never succeed. You think you got all the main players, when you captured Jupiter the first time? Do you really think Jupiter would hand over everyone in the operation?" She laughed

199

such an evil laugh that it sent cold chills over them.

"You won't have to worry about any of that, Miss Baker," Wade said. "You'll be dead. We're going for the death penalty. You'll be strapped down and given a lethal cocktail in a needle."

All color drained from her face. "You won't do that. You didn't give Jupiter the death penalty and she was the head of the whole operation. I'm just a lieutenant. But I can give you some names."

"We don't need you, Miss Baker. Buzz and Winnie are in the other room singing like birds. No, I think we'll just get you taken out of society for good. Just end your miserable life."

"Wait a minute, wait a minute. They know nothing. They can't help you. I know where headquarters is, how it got started, and all the main people. I'll give you all of that, if you give me the same deal you gave Jupiter, life in a mental hospital for the criminally insane. I'll even let your wife, Judith, study me like she did Jupiter."

Wade turned to John Pepper. "Sheriff, you want to put her in a cell, so we can discuss this?"

Pepper got up, reaching for his keys on his belt. "Come on, Ma'am," he said. "Let me show you to your room."

CHAPTER 38

Ruth Winslow, aka Miss Baker, sat on the cot in her cell. She was trying to come up with some names. She wished she hadn't mentioned Jupiter. She had never met Jupiter, but had read about her in the paper. That's where she had come up her idea. She had been about to lose the house that had been in her family for generations. Buzz was easy to recruit. He had been her chauffeur for years. When she had asked him if he wanted to make lots of money, he had agreed without hesitation. His wife, Winnie would do whatever he said.

At first she had been limited to grabbing run-aways. It was Winnie who suggested that Ruth ride the bus and look for kids on the run. Once she had the operation going for awhile, she was contacted by Pedro. He had kids to sell. Buzz had met him in a bar and given him her phone number. After that, they had regular shipments. *I could give them Pedro. He doesn't matter. I sure shouldn't have mentioned Jupiter. I could never be in her class.*

When the sheriff came and got her, she was ready to talk, to make a plea bargain. As soon as she was seated and Wade had turned on the tape recorder, Ruth Winslow said, "I never met Jupiter. I did admire her and, after reading about her in the newspaper, I got the idea for my own operation."

"Sounds like you have nothing to bargain with," Wade said.

"I can give you Buzz and Winnie."

"We already have them. They've already confessed. Come on, Miss Baker, if that's your real name, you can do better than a couple of servants. What's your real name? Let's start with that."

She stared at Wade and looked like she was trying to make up her mind about something. Then in a shaky voice, she said, "My name is Ruth Winslow."

"Hey, I know who you are," Sheriff Pepper said. "I knew you looked familiar." Turning to Wade and Judith, he said, "This is Judge Winslow's widow."

Wade and Judith looked at each other and shrugged.

"It was big news down here," the sheriff continued. "Judge Winslow was caught with his hands in the cookie jar. By doing a little creative bookkeeping, he became a rich man. When he was finally caught, the coward blew his brains out."

Ruth started crying. In her helpless old lady voice, she said, "I was broke after he died. I had to find a way to keep my house. It's been in my family for generations."

Judith laughed a bitter laugh. "You want us to feel sorry for you? You think that selling kids is all right because you were broke? There are plenty of people who are broke who don't sell kids. There are thousands of poor people who are honest upright citizens…"

Wade put his hand on Judith's arm. She quit talking. Turning to Mrs. Winslow, he said, "Your tears are wasted on us, Ma'am. How did you get the kids you were bringing in and how do you go about selling them?"

"A lawyer friend of my late husband has an office in Miami. He handles the adoptions for me. His name is Roscoe Wacoal. The man who sells the kids to me lives in Mexico, his name is Pedro, but I don't know his last name. He brings kids over who have no one. We're really doing them a favor."

Wade looked confused. "Are you telling us that you're selling kids for illegal adoption, that you're not running a pedophile ring like Jupiter?"

Taking a lacy handkerchief out of her purse, Ruth said, "I was going to take over where Jupiter left off, but then, when I got Mr. Wacoal involved, he wanted no part of that. He was willing to help people who couldn't have kids, though."

"Do you have anything else to say?"

"What's going to happen to me?" she asked.

CHAPTER 39

Ruth Winslow was taken to Miami where she was tried and convicted of child trafficking. Roscoe Wacoal was convicted of illegal adoption. The police are still looking for Pedro. The border patrol is on the lookout for him as well. Ms. Winslow was sentenced to 12 years in Raiford. With good behavior, she should be out in six. Mr. Wacoal was sentenced to twenty-five.

After wrapping up the case, that Wade called The Fake Jupiter Case, Granny and Annie returned to Enid, Texas. Wade, Judith, Sam and Billy made their way back to Monroe Beach to visit Sarah and Robert and to catch them up on all that had happened since they left Key Largo. Sam agreed to stay with Robert and Sarah, after Judith called Judge Hemmings. Robert and Sarah were granted temporary custody of her. After a short visit, they said tearful goodbyes. Out of character, Sam hugged Billy, allowing herself to cry on his shoulder.

"I'll always remember you, Sam," Billy said as his tears dropped on top of her head.

Billy, Wade and Judith then headed to Nashville, so that Billy could testify at his dad's trial.

CHAPTER 40

On the long trip from Monroe Beach to Nashville, Billy was quiet, staring out the window, watching the scenery go by. Judith and Wade didn't try to draw him out, but left him alone to sort out his thoughts and emotions. They took the scenic route, going through the mountains instead of traveling the freeway. Billy remembered what it had been like to hike through the hills and how scared he had been. *I hope I can help my daddy. I don't want to be on my own anymore. If Daddy gets out of prison and marries a mean woman again, I won't say a word. I'll take it like a man til I'm grown up. I won't tell Daddy and I won't run away. I'll be a good boy. I don't want to be in foster care. I don't want to live with Judith and Wade, even though I love them. I want to be with my daddy.*

As they were driving into Macon, Georgia, Judith turned around in her seat and looked at Billy. He looked so lost in thought she regretted interrupting him.

When he made eye contact, she asked, "Are you hungry?"

Billy nodded and Wade spotted a McDonald's. Pulling into the parking lot, he said, "Let's go inside instead of driving through. We have plenty of time."

Billy mostly played with his food. Judith studied him for a few minutes and then put her hand on his arm. He jumped.

Pulling her hand back, she said, "I really don't think you have anything to worry about, honey. I talked to his lawyer this morning before you got up. She doesn't think your dad will have to serve any time. He may have to do community service and take anger management classes. She's asked me to do the psychological evaluation and testify in court. I have a good feeling about this, Billy."

He searched her eyes and knew she was telling the truth. He began to relax. After lunch, they got back on the road and arrived in Nashville five and a half hours later. Wade checked them into a nice hotel near the courthouse so they could walk. They had two days before the trial began.

"Billy, what do you want to do? We have two days to kill. You want to go to the Grand Ole Opry and see some stars?"

"Nah, I already did that a bunch of times. I want to go see my Daddy."

"Is that possible?" Judith asked Wade. "Does it depend on the state?"

"It does. Why don't you call Ms. Foley and ask her."

Billy watched as Judith talked to his dad's attorney. When she hung up, she gave a thumbs up. Jumping up and down, Billy squealed.

"When can we go?" Billy asked in a loud voice.

"Visiting hours are over for today," Judith said. "We have to wait until 9:00 a.m. tomorrow. But, I'll tell you what. They have a heated pool here. Let's go for a swim."

The next morning Billy was up before the crack of dawn. He crawled out of his bed and peeked into the room where Judith and Wade were sleeping. He pulled the curtain back and gazed down at the pool. *I could take a dip while I'm waiting.*

When Judith woke up at 7:30, she tiptoed to Billy's room. Panicking, she shook wade. "Honey wake up. Where's Billy?"

"He's around somewhere," Wade said in a sleepy voice. "What are you doing up so early?"

"It's 7:30, Wade. Get up. We've got to find Billy."

"Relax, Judith. He's not going to run this time. He's around here somewhere." Wade got up yawning. He walked over to the window and looked down. Laughing, he said to Judith, "Come here, Sweetheart. Billy's trying to dive."

What she saw made Judith giggle. "He looks just like a frog jumping into the water. Look at his legs."

They watched until he got out and said something to a lady lying on a lounge chair. She looked at her watch and answered. He grabbed his towel and started drying off while walking toward the building.

"Let's order room service," Wade said. "That way, we can eat while we get ready."

CHAPTER 41

Male inmates awaiting trial in Nashville are held at the Davidson County Criminal Justice Center. They are allowed two visitors at a time. Judith asked to accompany Billy. She wanted to observe the interaction between father and son. Linda Foley had asked Judith to do a full psychological evaluation of Kenneth and observing him with his kid would help in her evaluation.

Billy and Judith sat side by side facing a window. Soon Kenneth sat down in front of them and picked up the phone on the wall. Billy grinned form ear to ear as he picked up the phone on the other side.

"Hey, Daddy." Billy was so chocked up he could hardly speak.

Kenneth put his palm on the glass and Billy did the same. Kenneth closed his eyes then blinked back tears of joy. Watching them, Judith was so moved she felt tears stinging her eyes.

"Daddy, this is Dr. Judith McCain."

Judith smiled. "Mr. Sunders, I'm so glad to finally meet you. I guess Ms. Foley has already talked to you about me doing a psychological workup on you."

"It's good to meet you too, Dr. McCain. Linda told me that you would be doing a psychological evaluation. Just what does this evaluation entail?"

"Please, call me Judith. I'll be giving you a series of psychological tests. We'll talk a little, and then I'll give my opinion to Linda. We'll talk about it later. I don't want to take up any of your time with Billy, today. They only gave him 45 minutes."

Judith watched the interaction between father and son. She could see how special their relationship was. They talked excitedly, catching each other up on what had been happening. She was looking forward to working with Kenneth.

When the 45 minutes was almost over, Judith said, "Kenneth, don't worry about Billy. We'll take good care of him until you get out. I'll see you later this afternoon, around 2:00, to begin the evaluation."

"Thanks you so much for everything, Judith. I'm so glad Billy has y'all. I was so worried about him."

Judith put her hand on Billy's shoulder. "You ready to go, sport?"

"I'm ready. Bye, Daddy.

CHAPTER 42

After having lunch with Wade and Billy, Judith left them at the pool and headed for the jail. She couldn't wait to get started, having always enjoyed working with a new client. Her briefcase was stuffed with the tests needed for the evaluation: The TAT, the Rorschach, the MMPI and the WISC. She also had pencils, sketch pad, crayons and paint. Art therapy helps to get to the subconscious faster. There was a meeting scheduled with Linda Foley when the evaluation was completed.

Judith checked in at the front of the jail, where she had to leave her purse. She was then taken to a room with windows on three sides. As she was laying out the materials for the testing, Kenneth was brought in. She was glad to see that he wasn't shackled. She started to shake his hand and then remembered, from past experiences, that she wasn't allowed.

"I'll be right outside if you need me, Dr. McCain," the guard said. Before she could

reply, he walked out, closing the door
behind him. He and another guard stood and
watched through the window.

"How are you, Kenneth?" Judith asked
while getting the materials out of her
briefcase.

"To tell you the truth, Doctor, I'm a little
nervous," he said.

"Of course you are. There's no need to
be. What's your biggest fear?"

He gave a shaky laugh. "I'm afraid
you'll think I'm crazy."

"To put your mind at ease, I know you're
not."

"Oh, you already know that?"

"Yep."

Kenneth let out a long sigh of relief.

Judith laughed. "Feel better, now?"
When he nodded she began. "I'm going to
show you some photographs and I want you
to tell me a story to go with each one."

It was after 7:00 when Judith got back to
the hotel. The three had supper together, and
then Judith shut herself in their bedroom
while Wade and Billy watched a movie.
Spreading all the tests and artwork out on
the bed, she picked up the MMPI, the most

reliable and the most used instrument for testing personality. Judith always started with that when evaluating a client.

She was glad to see the psychopathology and personality disorders scales were very low and that the lie scale was low. The anxiety, depression, dependency and fears scales were high. She expected that. Aggressiveness was high but dominance was low. She smiled when she saw that the family values and psychotherapy suitability scales were high.

The IQ test, WISC, showed high intelligence with score of 135. The stories he told for the TAT showed high family values but intense fear. The Rorschach (ink blot) test showed fears and feelings of inadequacy.

Judith was studying the paintings when Wade opened the door. "It's after midnight. How much longer are you going to be?"

"Oh, I didn't realize it was so late," she said as she began to gather up her notes and tests.

Wade picked up one of the ink blots, turning it upside down and then sideways. "This looks like a butterfly."

She took it from him.

"Am I right?"

She laughed. "There is no right or wrong answer."

"This is the strangest honeymoon I've ever had."

"You've never had a honeymoon before, Wade."

"That's true. Are you too tired for a little honeymoon sample tonight?"

"Definitely not. Just let me get a quick shower."

"I'll join you."

CHAPTER 43

"Linda said that today and probably tomorrow will be jury selection," Judith said as she ran the brush through her hair. "Then the prosecution will begin calling their witnesses. She said it will probably be sometime next week before Billy will need to be there."

"Well, you might as well go to Fall Creek Falls with us. You know they're not going to let you in there before you testify, Judith."

"I know that, Wade. I can watch the jury selection though. I want to get a good look at the jury. We can do something together after that and before the prosecution presents its case." She kissed him goodbye. "Y'all have fun today."

Billy was so excited to be going to Fall Creek Falls with Wade. He had been there with his dad many times. He loved hiking down to the falls and he liked being with Wade. He was so glad he wasn't on the run anymore and that his daddy would hopefully soon be free.

Wade was just hanging up the phone when he came into the living room. "Looks like you're ready to go," he said, smiling at Billy. "I just talked to the kitchen and they're packing us a lunch. We're having ham sandwiches, potato salad, soft drinks and cookies. We can grab a snack for breakfast on the way. How long did you say it takes to get there?" he asked, looking at his watch.

"About two hours. Me and my dad always stop at McDonalds and get an egg McMuffin and chocolate milk."

"We can do that, if you want."

Judith sat near the back of the courtroom and studied the defense attorney, Linda Foley and the assistant district attorney, Rachael Montgomery. Besides being interested in human behavior, she was especially interested in the way in which they questioned the jury. They each had their own unique style. Ms. Foley was tall, soft spoken and deliberate. Ms. Montgomery was petite, moved with nervous energy and spoke in a clipped manner. She fired off questions to potential jury members and either accepted or rejected them quickly. Linda Foley paused often while studying each person before making up her mind.

Judith was surprised when the jury selection was completed before the end of the first day. Judge Bernard was a heavy set black man with a full head of white hair. When the jury had its 12 members and alternates, he looked at his watch and said, "Ms. Montgomery, do you want to make your opening statement now or would you rather wait until tomorrow?"

Standing she said, "If it pleases the court, I'd like to wait until tomorrow."

"Very well," he said. "Court will convene tomorrow morning at 9:00 a.m."

Kenneth Sunders was taken back to his cell and Judith waited for Linda Foley while everyone was leaving. She watched the attorney pack up her briefcase, then turn and wave. Judith waved back and they walked toward each other.

"Do you want to have some lunch?" Linda asked. "I'm starving. I was too nervous to eat breakfast."

"Yeah, let's have lunch."

As they were walking out of the building, Judith asked, "Are you always too nervous to eat before going to court?"

Linda laughed. "I wouldn't know since this is my first case. I want to win this case so badly. Not just because it is my first case and I want to make a name for myself, but because I really like Kenneth Sunders. I think he is a good man. I mean, I know he has a drinking problem and some anger issues, but he can work on those, right?"

They walked out onto the sidewalk and Linda led the way down a couple of blocks to a small restaurant. After they were seated, Judith said, "To answer your question, yes. In fact, my recommendation to the court will be for Kenneth to be required to go to AA and to take anger management classes. I will also recommend family therapy for him and Billy."

A waiter came and Judith ordered a Caesar salad and a glass of sweet iced tea. Linda ordered rare steak, baked potato, salad, and a glass of red wine. Judith wondered how she stayed so slim. While they waited for their food, Judith opened her briefcase and took out her notes.

As she was explaining the tests results to Linda, their food arrived and Judith moved her notes over to the side. Linda cut into her steak and chewed while staring off into space. When she swallowed, she took a sip of wine. "Listen, Judith, before you go any farther, in Tennessee, the burden of proof is on the State. What I mean by that is the prosecutor is required to show the defendant's willful intent in order to prove guilt. That makes things a little easier for us, but what we need to do to strengthen our case is to present a defense of irresistible impulse."

"I feel that we can do that easily," Judith said. "I can testify that Kenneth is not insane. None of the tests show any psychopathology. We can show that he does know right from wrong and that he was unable to control his actions at the time he killed Rose. There's just one thing, Linda. You need to subpoena me to testify. Otherwise, the FBI is probably not going to allow me to testify. They might claim that it's a conflict of interest, even though I was only peripherally involved in the case."

Linda nodded. "I can do that." Taking another sip of wine, she raised her glass. "To our team. To our winning team."

"Here, here," Judith said, raising her glass of iced tea.

CHAPTER 44

Kenneth sat at the defense table listening to his neighbors, from the trailer park, testify about the fights they had heard and witnessed between him and Rose. He felt ashamed. It was disgusting to think what Billy must have gone through night after night. No wonder the poor kid had run away. *God, if you help me get out of here, I promise to be a good father. I promise to quit drinking. I promise to learn to control my anger. I want to make Billy proud of me. I want to be a good role model for him. He needs a daddy who is there for him, not a buddy.*

"The prosecution rests," he suddenly heard Ms. Montgomery say. He sat up straighter and breathed a sigh of relief. Linda had given him hope and now it was their turn.

"The defense may call the first witness," the judge said. He looked like he was trying to suppress a yawn. Kenneth hoped the jury had become bored with the endless line of witnesses the prosecution had paraded before the court.

"Thank you, your honor," Linda said. "I call Billy Sunders to the stand."

An officer of the court got Billy out of the hallway. Judith had helped Billy dress that morning. He was wearing a pair of dress pants, a dress shirt, and his new navy blue parka. He walked to the stand with confidence. The bailiff put a large cushion on the chair, swore him in and he sat down. He looked over at his dad, smiled and waved.

After he was sworn in, the judge leaned over toward where he was sitting and asked, "Billy, do you know the difference between the truth and a lie?"

Billy looked at the judge and frowned. "Yes, sir, I do."

The judge leaned back and smiled. "You may proceed, counselor."

Linda smiled at him. "Hello, Billy. How are you doing today?"

"I'm fine."

"Do you remember when your dad married Rose? How old were you?"

"I was five. I remember when they got married. Dad was happy that day. Rose was nice then."

"Did Rose ever hit you?"

"Well, not at first. She was real nice at first. She would even play games with me."

"And when did that change, Billy?"

"When I broke her jewelry box. I just wanted to look at her shiny things. She showed them to me before. I dropped it and it broke."

"And what did she do?"

"She slapped me."

"And were there other times, Billy?"

"Yes, she got meaner and meaner. If I spilt anything, she would hit me."

"Where did she hit you, Billy?"

"Sometimes in the kitchen, sometimes in the yard…"

"No, Billy." Linda interrupted him. "I mean, where on your body did she hit you and what did she hit you with?"

"Oh, when I broke her box, she slapped me in the face. She hit me with anything she had in her hand. One time she was frying some pork chops, so she had a big, long fork and she hit me in the face with it. It cut my cheek. See, the scar?" Billy said, turning his head around so that Linda could see the scar on his cheek.

Kenneth watched his precious little boy as he described the abuse he had endured at the hands of the woman he had married and brought into the trailer. He remembered that cut on Billy's cheek. Billy had told him he had fallen on a sharp rock. *Why didn't he tell me about Rose hitting him?*

"Why didn't you tell your dad about any of this abuse, Billy?" Linda Foley asked.

"She said if I told him, she would hurt me real bad. She said Daddy wouldn't believe me over her anyway because Daddy loved her better than me." Billy's bottom lip started trembling and tears welled up in his eyes.

As Linda was giving him time to compose himself, Ms. Montgomery jumped up. "Your honor, I feel badly for Billy, but Rose is not the one on trial here. I object to the defense trying to gain sympathy from the jury."

"Overruled, please continue, Ms. Foley."

"Thank you, your honor. Billy would you like some water?"

He shook his head, and then remembered that he was supposed to say everything out loud. "No," he said. Sitting up straighter, he prepared for the question he knew was coming next.

"Billy, tell us about the night you ran away. You were on a camping trip with your dad and Rose, right? Why did you run?"

"We had gone camping. Rose said it was to bring the family together. At first it was fun. We went fishing together and cooked the fish over the camp fire. Later that night, they started drinking and fighting again. I knew it wasn't going to get any better. I thought that if I left, maybe they would get along."

"Weren't you scared out in the woods all by yourself?"

"Nah, my dad had taught me how to survive in the wilderness. Before he married Rose, we used to camp out without a tent. But I had my own tent that night. I took it with me."

Kenneth was amazed at his little boy as he described his hike through the mountains, about his stay with Maw and Elvis after he had fallen off the trail and hit his head. *My son is an amazing kid. He's a survivor. But he shouldn't have had to survive. He should have been out playing like other little boys.*

If I get out of this, I'll make it up to you, Billy. I promise.

He looked at the jury. They seemed to be hanging onto Billy's every word.

"After they put Miss Baker in jail, Judith and Wade brought me up here to help my daddy," he concluded.

"Redirect," The judge said.

Ms. Montgomery stood. "I have no questions, your honor."

The judge looked at his watch. It's 11:45. I think this is a good place to take a lunch break. We'll reconvene at 1:00 p.m. Everyone stood as the jury and then the judge filed out.

CHAPTER 45

"You did so well, Billy," Linda said as she squeezed his hand. They were eating at a deli around the corner from the courthouse.

Billy liked Linda and wished his dad would marry someone like her. She smelled good too. He kept leaning over close so he could smell her. He wished he could hug her or that she would hug him.

Linda took a bite of her pastrami sandwich. Chewing while staring out the window, she was thinking about the afternoon session. Then taking a few sips of her iced tea, she said, "Judith, I had, at first, thought to bring you in to testify after Billy, but I think I'll let Kenneth go next and then you. That way, you can make the recommendations we talked about."

"Is it wise to put Kenneth on the stand?" Judith asked. "I'm worried about his anger. What if he loses it during cross-examination? You know Rachael Montgomery is going to goad him to try to make him lose control."

"I know. I tried to tell him that. But he insisted. It is his legal right to take the stand in his own defense. I can't talk him out of it."

"It'll be okay," Billy said. "My dad can handle it. He's sober now. He only gets mad when he's drunk. You'll see. He'll do good."

Judith and Linda glanced at each other and smiled.

Looking at her watch, Linda said, "Where did the time go? We've got to hurry. I don't want the judge to charge me with contempt. I'm glad we paid when we got our food. Now we can just go."

They made it in time, but not by much. Kenneth was already seated at the defense table. Billy was now allowed to sit behind his daddy since he had already testified. Linda was getting papers out of her briefcase when they were told to rise. The judge walked in, sat down, and looked at Linda. "Is the defense ready to proceed?" he asked.

"We're ready, your honor. I call Kenneth Sunders to the stand."

Linda watched him walk to the stand. He had lost his beer belly since she had first met him. He was wearing the expensive suit

Judith had bought him and he looked handsome sobered and cleaned up.

"Are you ready to proceed, counselor?" The judge said and she realized that she had been lost in fantasies about Kenneth Sunders. She looked at the jury. They were watching her and she could feel her face turn red. *What am I going to do? Blow my first case because I'm suddenly attracted to the defendant?*

Taking a paper from the table, that had nothing to do with questioning the witness, but everything to do with giving her time to compose herself, she walked to the podium. He had already been sworn in.

"Mr. Sunders, where is Billy's real mother?"

"She died giving birth."

"So, you took care of Billy by yourself until you married Rose?"

"Except for a few months here and there when I had a live-in girlfriend."

"So, Billy was left with whomever you happened to be dating?"

Kenneth dropped his head. He knew that looked bad for him. He wondered how his priorities had gotten so messed up, that he would leave his little boy with whomever he happened to be sleeping with at the time. The booze had clouded his mind, but he couldn't blame everything on alcohol. Since he had been in jail, he had time to sober up. His could now see everything clearly. He had been a terrible father.

"The witness will answer the question," Judge Barnard said.

"I'm sorry, your honor. May I talk without the questions?"

The judge took a deep breath and looked at Linda. She nodded. "It's not the way things are usually done," he said, "but I'll allow it."

Ms. Montgomery jumped to her feet. "I object, your honor. You've given the defense way too much leeway…"

"Sit down, Ms. Montgomery. You'll get a chance to cross. Your objection is overruled."

As she sat, she threw her hands up in the air. The judge glared at her. Then turning toward Kenneth, he said, "Please go on, Mr. Sunders."

Kenneth looked at Billy. "After Jessica, Billy's mother, died I had a hard time even getting up in the mornings. I never let myself cry like I wanted to. I thought I had to be strong for Billy. Instead of grieving, I started drinking. I'm ashamed to admit it, but I went out to bars just about every night, after Billy went to sleep. Sometimes I would bring a woman home with me and get her to stay with Billy the next morning, so I could go to work. I had a regular job at the time.

"I later tried working for myself as a handyman, so that I could be with Billy as much as possible. I even took him on some jobs with me. Sometimes, the woman of the house, where I was working at the time, looked after him while I fixed whatever needed fixing. By the time I met Rose, I was seriously considering finding a mother for Billy. Rose seemed like a kind, responsible woman. She was funny and loved Billy right away, or that's what she said and what I believed. After watching her with Billy I asked her to marry me.

"Things seemed to be working out all right at first, but then Rose started drinking. Then I started drinking. After awhile, the fights started and I can't tell you who started the fights or what they were about. Now that

I've sobered up, looking back, it all seems so stupid. Billy needed us and we only thought of ourselves.

"I love Billy. I want to a chance to be a good father to him. I'm sorry I killed Rose. She wasn't a good person, but she didn't deserve to die. I was in such a rage after Billy ran away. Then when I found out that Rose knew he had run away and didn't tell me, I lost it. I snapped."

Kenneth put his head in his hands and cried. The jury looked at Billy. He too was crying, his shoulders shaking. Several people in the jury and in the congregation were crying. The prosecutor stared coldly at Kenneth. Linda took a handkerchief out of her jacket pocket and wiped her eyes.

"Mr. Sunders," Linda said, "After you killed Rose you ran. Did you run to escape prosecution?"

Kenneth looked surprised. "I had to find my boy, to make sure he was all right. I couldn't look for him if I was in jail."

"I have no further questions," Linda said.

The prosecutor looked unsure as she rose from her seat. By the time she got to the podium she had gained her confidence. "Mr.

Sunders that was a very touching story you just told. You obviously gained the sympathy of the jury. I noticed some of them were crying…"

"Ms. Montgomery, do you have a question for this witness?" the judge asked.

"I do, you honor."

"Then ask it."

"Mr. Sunders, do you believe you shouldn't be punished for committing murder? Do you believe that, just because you say you're sorry, that you should get off scot free?"

Kenneth sighed, "No ma'am, I don't…"

"Do you think that anyone can commit a crime, come in here and say they're sorry, and get the jury to cry, and then they get a free pass? Is that what you believe, Mr. Sunders? You didn't come home drunk, lose control and kill your wife Mr. Sunders. You planned it out. We all know that it was premeditated murder."

The judge interrupted. "Are you trying to change the charge at this late a date, Ms. Montgomery?"

"I'm sorry, your honor," she said. "The charge is still manslaughter. I got a little carried away."

"You will not get 'carried away' again. Do you understand counselor?"

"Yes sir, I do."

"Then please continue."

Kenneth knew she had been trying to get him mad. Linda had warned him about this. He did feel angry, but Judith had told him that anger was alright, it's what you do with that feeling that's important. He chose to smile. It seemed to confuse the prosecutor.

"Why are you smiling, Mr. Sunders? Aren't you angry?"

"Yes, Ma'am, I am."

"Mr. Sunders. Let's talk about the night you killed Rose. I read the statement you gave the FBI. You stated that you drove home from the police station, parked the car in front of your trailer, and went to the back yard. There you drank and thought about killing her. You came into the kitchen and noticed that she was drunk. The empty bottle of vodka was on the counter. Tell the jury what you did next, Mr. Sunders."

"I had been looking at the swing set in the back yard, worrying about Billy. Having just found out that Rose knew Billy had run away and didn't tell me, I became more and more angry. Worried about my son, I came in and found her drunk. It was like the last straw. I snapped. Without thinking, I snatched the bottle off the counter and hit her across the face." Kenneth again put his head in his hands and wept.

"But you didn't stop there, did you Mr. Sunders? You then grabbed an iron skillet off the stove and continued to hit her in the face and head until she was dead. And then you ran. You weren't thinking about your son when you ran. You ran because you didn't want to go to jail. Isn't that true, Mr. Sunders?"

Kenneth sat slumped over, head in hands, sobbing. It was all that could be heard. Then Ms. Montgomery said in a quiet voice, "I have no more questions."

Kenneth pulled a handkerchief out of his pocket and wiped his eyes. He looked around as if he couldn't remember where he was.

"You may step down, Mr. Sunders," the judge said.

When he took his seat, Linda patted his arm. Leaning over she whispered, "You did great. Try not to worry. Hold your head up."

The judge ran his hand through his hair. "I think this is a good place to call it a day. Court will convene at 9:00 a.m. tomorrow.

CHAPTER 46

"I don't know about you, Judith, but I'm looking forward to this honeymoon being over and getting on with married life," Wade said as he dried off from the shower. "I mean, now that we've caught the bad guys, the fun's over for me. How much longer do you think the trial will last?"

"Well, I'll be testifying tomorrow morning, and then the jury will go into deliberations. It's hard to tell, Wade. I'm sorry, honey. I know this is boring for you, trying to keep an eight year old boy occupied all day."

"That's okay. I can hang in there. I think I'll go down to the gift shop and get a paperback to read by the pool while Billy swims today. That should pass the time."

Judith closed her briefcase she had been packing. Giving Wade a quick peck on the cheek, she said, "I'll see you later."

Judith and Linda had agreed to meet at 8:00 a.m., in one of the small rooms off the courtroom, to go over her testimony. She found Linda sitting in one of the chairs with her feet on the table, talking out loud. Judith stood at the door. She didn't want to interrupt, but Linda saw her and sat up, putting the pages aside.

"Hi, Judith. I was just going over my closing statement. I'm so nervous about it."

"I'm sure you'll do fine." Judith began spreading out the food on the table.

Linda grabbed her coffee and took a big gulp. "A man's life is at stake here, Judith. Not just any man, but a man I've grown to like a lot."

"Like a lot, huh?" Judith said and winked.

Linda shrugged.

Judith sat down and opened her briefcase, getting out her notes. "Okay, the way I understand this, from what you've said, we need to show two things. One is that Kenneth is not insane. That's easily done. All I have to do is to talk about the MMPI. It's the most reliable psychological test there is. His shows no psychopathology or personality disorders. You said that the second thing we need to show is that he knows right from wrong, but was unable to control his actions at the time he killed Rose. This part will be a little more difficult to show, but if we give the jury a long list of stressors leading up to that moment when he snapped, I really think we can pull it off."

Judith took a big bite of her bagel, chewed, swallowed and took a sip of coffee. "For Kenneth, the stress started the day Billy was born, when his wife died giving birth. The loss of a spouse is the second biggest stressor on the stress scale, the loss of a child being number one. He never grieved her death. Carrying around unresolved grief is a major stressor. The stress continued when had to constantly try to find someone to take care of Billy. Then he finally thinks he's found someone to take care of him, but she turns out to be a drunk who cares nothing for the child. When Billy ran away and Kenneth found out that Rose knew all along, he felt betrayed by her. It was too much for him and he snapped. This is just an outline of the way I'll present it in court."

Linda breathed a sigh of relief. "I feel better already. This is going to make my closing statement easier too. I'll reiterate what you said about the stressors. I have a good feeling about this."

"Me, too." Judith looked at her watch. "Show time."

During cross examination, Ms. Montgomery tried her best to trip Judith up, but Judith had done this many times and no one had ever been able to sway her. Judith was surprised when she stepped down from the witness stand and looked at her watch. She had only been up there a half hour. Judith thought Linda did a marvelous job in her closing statement. When the judge sent the jury to deliberate, they were dismissed for lunch.

"Let's go have a drink," Linda said, as they exited the courthouse.

"Yeah, let's."

Three drinks later, they were looking at their watches every few seconds. "I think this is the hardest part of the whole thing," Linda said. "What's going to happen to Billy if Kenneth is sent to prison?"

"Billy will come live with us in Houston, but he's not going to prison, Linda. Really, I have a good feeling about this."

The afternoon dragged on. At 6:00 p.m. Linda's cell phone rang. "We'll be right there. The jury has reached a verdict."

Judith's heart skipped a beat. They were silent as they walked toward the courthouse.

Judith sat behind Linda. When the jury filed in Judith studied their faces trying to read them, but was unsuccessful. When the judge told the defendant to rise, Judith saw Kenneth take Linda's hand. Judith held her breath as the verdict was being read.

"We, the jury find the defendant guilty of manslaughter."

"No!" Billy cried, tears streaming down his face.

Judith pulled Billy against her, smoothing his sweaty hair off his face and wiping his eyes with a tissue. He sobbed quietly against her chest. Her heart broke for him.

Thanking them, the judge dismissed the jury. Linda was patting Kenneth's hand and whispering in his ear. He was nodding his head. The judge told everyone to be seated, except Mr. Sunders. Judith held Billy tightly as he stared at the judge. She could feel his heart pounding.

"Mr. Sunders, the jury has found you guilty of manslaughter. I am sentencing you to three years, 6 months of which will be served at Charles Bass Correctional Complex, and two and a half years probation. While at Bass, you will attend their anger management classes and AA meetings. When you get out, and are on probation, you will attend family therapy with your son, Billy. Do you have any questions, Mr. Sunders?"

"What's going to happen to my boy, while I'm in prison?"

"He will be a charge of the state. He will be placed in foster care until you get out."

Billy's worst fear was about to come true. He was going to have to stay with foster parents. He was scared.

The judge looked around the room, and then he stood. "Court is adjourned," he said.

Billy watched as they took his dad out in shackles. He was too scared to cry. The Linda turned to them and said, "Billy, a case worker is on the way to pick you up. You will have to stay in a shelter while they try to find a foster home for you. In the meantime, Judith and Wade will file for temporary.

"Is that what you want, Billy?" Judith asked. "Do you want to come live with Wade and me in Houston until your dad gets out?"

Billy grinned and nodded.

Judith and Wade returned to Houston with Billy. Kenneth was released five months later. Wade and Judith took Billy back to Nashville and watched the happy reunion of father and son. A year and a half later, Judith was surprised to get a letter from Kenneth Sunders.

Dear Judith,

It has been a year since I was released from prison. I want to thank you again for your help. Linda and I have been seeing each other. Last night I asked her to be my wife and Billy's mother. We are overjoyed that she accepted. I got my one year sobriety chip from AA last week. I completed the anger management classes on the outside, but Billy and I are still in family therapy. We had a lot of grief work to do. I feel like a heavy weight has been lifted off my shoulders. Billy is thriving. He's making straight A's. He says he's going to be a psychologist like you. Linda and I would like you to be our matron of honor. The wedding is November 22nd. I hope I'm giving you enough time.

Love,
Kenneth

Other books by Peggy Holloway:

The Judith McCain mysteries:
Blood on White Wicker
Portrait on Wicker
Terror on the Beach
Jupiter Returns
Monroe Beach

3037
Time and Time Again (The sequel to 337)

Double Shock (Suspense/thriller)

Southern Greed (Romantic Suspense)

The Christmas tree Inheritance
(A Christmas mystery)

The Answers Are Within
(Self –help)

A Life of Confusion (Memoires)

http://authorpeggyholloway.webs.com

Peggyholloway62@yahoo.com